THE SELF-DIRECTED SHIFT

RICKEY LEWIS

"A personal development & growth book about choice, direction and principles that lead to the life you've always wanted to live."

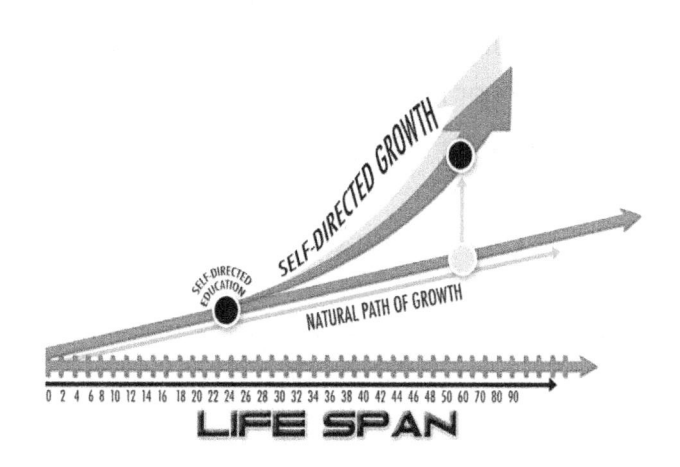

SELF-DIRECTED GROWTH

SELF-DIRECTED EDUCATION

NATURAL PATH OF GROWTH

0 2 4 6 8 10 12 14 16 18 20 22 24 26 28 30 32 34 36 38 40 42 44 46 48 50 60 70 80 90

LIFE SPAN

DEDICATION

Dedicated to the life and memory of Armand Francis Xavier Theriault, SVD.

"Father T" was a Godsend. He was the right person at the right time to come into a sixteen-year-old confused boy's life and help him become a man. The direction my life took because of his presence and guidance has produced and will continue to produce great fruits of success on the tree of life. Owe him the world.

ACKNOWLEDGEMENTS

There are many people whom made this book possible. Thank you to all of the people who have helped shape and mold me through the process of this project. So many friends and family members gave words of encouragement and inspiration whether it was in person or through my social media platforms. Each and every one of you gave me the energy to keep pressing on. That comment, like and share made this book happen. I have to give a special thanks to Bruce Northridge for the initial editing and the countless hours of English lessons that wore my brain out. He helped bring my spoken word and story telling into a written form. There is no project I can complete without my home team. That team is my wife Lauren and my three sons Landon, Lathan and Larkin. Each one of them gives me the inspiration to be the best I can be. They give me the reasons to be great. The Queen's unconditional love and patience for the four of us boys, makes all things possible in the Lewis household.

FOREWORD

Allow me to introduce you to an amazing man who may be a novice writer to some, but brings inspiration, influence and guidance though his masterful writing. Rickey Lewis' intricate descriptions of how he has overcome odds and turned life's challenges into triumphs is yet another testament to his rightful place at the table. This body of work impeccably leads you into the kitchen of life, offering the reader a dish likened to a pot of gumbo. A splash of rejection, mixed with a dash of resilience is beautifully paired with a cup of determination and discipline. He carefully stirs a tablespoon of heartache and whisks in a few ounces of unconditional love providing the making of a tasty roux.

After the addition of life's lumps and bruises and several pounds of fresh love and success, the reader is now ready to indulge in a hearty meal. These ingredients of experiences and innumerable successes and losses are sure to leave an imprint on the world. Your print however, depends on your choices. Be them good, or not so good. Be them horrible or honorable, the imprint is yours and is a reflection of your choice.

Life will inevitably leave you with a few burns, bumps, and bruises, but you must never allow your faith to waiver. As you continue to add to life, you intentionally change the outcome. Welcome to the Self-Directed Shift.

Sonya Williams Barnes

Owner of Lockett Williams Mortuary, Inc.

She is the third generation of funeral service providers. She was elected and has served in the Mississippi State House representing District 119 since 2012.

TABLE OF CONTENTS

CHAPTER 1 -- 1

My Father and the Tale of Two Cousins ------------------------------------ 1

CHAPTER 2 ---12

Find a New Path & Create a Shift -- 12

CHAPTER 3 ---26

Belief and Thinking-- 26

CHAPTER 4 ---38

Happiness, Feelings & Emotions -- 38

CHAPTER 5 ---55

Success and Dreams-- 55

CHAPTER 6 ---66

Seeing Further Down the Road -- 66

CHAPTER 7 ---76

Strengthen Your Faith, Secure Your Life --------------------------------- 76

CHAPTER 8 ---85

Financial Intelligence --- 85

CHAPTER 9 — 113
Relational Beings — 113

CHAPTER 10 — 140
Parenting — 140

CHAPTER 11 — 150
Leading Following Mentoring — 150

CHAPTER 12 — 166
Fear, Failure & Excuses — 166

CHAPTER 13 — 176
The Self — 176

CHAPTER 14 — 191
Small Steps of Disciplined Actions — 191

CHAPTER 15 — 199
Character & Integrity — 199

CHAPTER 16 — 211
Find Your Purpose & Leave a Legacy — 211

CHAPTER 17 — 224
An Attitude of Gratitude — 224

CHAPTER 18 — 232

The Mind ---- 232

CHAPTER 19 ---- 239

This Can Be the End or Your Beginning ---- 239

INTRODUCTION

"Very few beings really seek knowledge in this world. Mortal or immortal, few really ask. On the contrary, they try to wring from the unknown the answers they have already shaped in their own minds -- justifications, confirmations, forms of consolation without which they can't go on. To really ask is to open the door to the whirlwind. The answer may annihilate the question and the questioner."

-Anne Rice

There are a number of reasons why this book was written. The most important reason is that this book was written especially for you, the reader. There is nothing more important to you than what you need to grow in every way you possibly can. Someone recommended this book to you for a specific reason. There must be something in here that a special person in your life thought you needed to read at this very moment in your life.

Maybe you are on a personal quest to find answers that may bring you closer to the life you truly want to live. This book was written for you because it is your starting point to the success that lies ahead for you. It may be the pit stop, where you refuel for the race you've already started some time ago. You are on a Self-directed Shift and you have no intention of getting off of the path that is producing the fruits of your life.

This book has been a long time coming. There are several reasons why I wrote it and you have become the benefactor. As a young third grader in school, I attended a school assembly where we were presented with a book written by a third grader. I was amazed. This was a kid just like me. He was the same age and he had a book that he had written and published! Up to that point in my life, I was under the impression that adults wrote and illustrated books. Right then, I knew that one day I would write a book. There were several attempts as a pre-teen but none ever came to fruition. It was one of the first major goals of my life and it was set before I even understood what goals were or the concept of goal setting.

As an adult I realized that I could not die without letting at least one of the books I have inside of me out. I feel that we all have a story to tell. Every one of us has at least one book to share. That book may never be written or published, but it is in there. We live extraordinary lives. Our eyes see amazing things that others miss. We hear a wonderful world of sounds that only we can describe. We have the ability to live on through our experiences told from generation to generation. What better way to preserve the message you wish to share than through the written word.

This book was written for my three sons. I owe them so much. I understand that their lives can be made or broken through my actions and interactions with them. They need to see their father accomplish goals, dreams and milestones that others may believe are too far to grasp, so that they may do the same. I can't just tell my kids that I have always wanted to write a book. I have to hand it to them and say, "This is the book your father has written".

My children need to read this book just as much as every man, woman, and child needs to read it. Everyone won't read it and there is no guarantee that those three Lewis boys will read past the first page. The information is there for them to choose to indulge or not. My job is to lead them to the water and hope that I have made them thirsty enough to drink.

This book was written because the world needs this information. It is a tool to reach more people through my purpose to educate those around me and those I come into contact with. We all need inspiration. We need to know that our potential can be fulfilled. This is a part of my plan to, as Mahatma Gandhi said, be the change I want to see in the world. It is an attempt to intentionally affect my family, community and as many people as I can through a positive assault on their minds and thought processes.

It was written because there is an excitement in my heart that I can't quite explain. I was brought back to life like Robert DeNiro in the movie *Awakenings*.

Being charged with new life from learning, I needed an outlet to share what has given me the vigor and vitality of growth and development. It is said that the best way to wake a man up is to get him learning again. The learning forced me to open up to people, new ideas and to writing. There was no doubt that this book would be written and published. I knew why but I didn't know when or how. It didn't matter! I was going to do it.

CHAPTER 1

My Father and the Tale of Two Cousins

"When one has not had a good father, one must create one."

- Friedrich Nietzsche

I have many fond memories of times spent with my father. But I would need another 36 years to share them all. However, I would like to share a few of those memorable moments that have shaped me into the person that I am today. My father had the uncanny ability to know when to encourage us, when to tell us no, when to reprimand us, when to console us, and when to say nothing at all. This is something that I am still trying to master as a father myself.

I have memories of my father making sacrifice after sacrifice in order to make sure that we had what we needed. Notice I said what we needed. If you know my father, he can at times be bit frugal. Like the time that we took a family vacation to Disney World. It was in the heat of the summer and the lines were extremely long to the rides. We must have been there for several hours and had grown hot, tired, thirsty, and hungry. We knew that the price of food was outrageous at Disney World, but we didn't expect Daddy would starve us. We begged him to buy us something to eat and something to drink. In his mind, he was thinking we can eat a lot cheaper once we leave the park (today I understand that logic). After much suffering and begging on our part, he finally gave in. He bought us one turkey leg to share among the 4 of us. To this day that was the best turkey leg I have ever had.

Another memory that I have that still lives on today is my memory of him teaching me to play tennis. As you probably know, my father introduced me to the game of tennis at a very young age. He spent countless hours working with me and preparing me to play the sport at a competitive level. Little did I know many of the life lessons that I learned would be taught on the tennis court. Another thing that I was not aware of then, that is crystal clear to me now, was the level of sacrifice and time he put into developing me as a player. As I look back at the time that we spent on the tennis court, this was a connection that would serve to strengthen our bond for the rest of our lives. Much of the time that we spent together took place on the courts of St. Stanislaus, The Gulfport Racquet Club, and countless tournaments around the state and the entire southeast. As a part of our training and practice we would often play against each other (you know, a little friendly competition). In the beginning he would beat me pretty bad and he never had mercy on me. Well...... the tables turned a bit when I reached 14, for this was the first time that I was able to record a victory against him. This was a huge accomplishment for me. Pops was the *real deal, and I had defeated him. It was that much more special to me because I knew that he had not let me win. This was yet another life lesson that he taught; the value of hard work and determination. We also spent a lot of time playing beside one another as a pretty formidable doubles team. The running joke is that he carried me in doubles when I was younger and he was stronger, now I carry him. But isn't that what life is all about?*

You know I often hear people say that my father and I share many of the same personality characteristics, mannerisms, logic, and interests. Both of us being tennis players and educators we sometimes encounter the same people, but at different times. It is a proud feeling to say that he is my father, and to hear the responses from the people that I am speaking to. If I had a penny for every time that someone told me what a great man he was I would be a very wealthy man. I have been blessed to have the opportunity to be raised by this man. Dad, if I can grow to be half the man that you are, my time on this earth will be well spent. I am proud to call you Daddy."

I wish that I could tell you that those were my words. I have never really picked up a tennis racket or played that sport competitively. My sports were baseball and football. I only saw my father a handful of times my entire life. Those were the words of my first cousin, Dr. Myron Bruce Labat, Jr. He was honoring his father, my mother's only brother and eldest of the nine Labat siblings. You see, this night is one that will forever be etched into my brain. It was a turning point, or one of those crossroads that we sometimes come to in our lives. It was the beginning of my Self-directed Shift. The setting was a church banquet hall filled with over one hundred and fifty family members and friends celebrating Myron senior's sixtieth birthday.

It became so surreal. I'm listening to these words, hearing others speak and watching the tears flow down his daughter's face as this great man is honored for the life he has lived and how he has truly touched, shaped and dramatically impacted the success of his children's lives. Looking around the room, I feel hopeless. At one point I know that I was the saddest soul in the building. People were laughing and I wanted to cry. Not tears of joy but of sorrow. It had dawned on me. I would never get an opportunity to honor my father. My father passed away years before this event and even if he hadn't, there wouldn't have been very much for me to say. My spiritual mentor and the closest figure to me, as a true father figure, had also passed away. Myron Jr. got to honor his father while he was alive. I wanted to do just that but the crazy thing is that I had no such person to thank for my success. Truthfully I didn't feel like much of a success anyway. I was getting by okay in life, but the success I had imagined and dreamed of had not been realized. My cousin -- now he was the success! He's just a year older than me and I've been looking up to him for as long as I can remember. We lived parallel lives on different planes I guess you could say. We really weren't much different. We had the same blood running through our veins. We were equally talented athletically and for the most part academically. The differences between us came down to choices. Remember that last sentence and that powerful word, CHOICE.

In our teens, I felt the need to attend every dance or social function whereas he chose the right ones. He was evaluating his life and contemplating Wants versus Needs. It is evident now that he was employing the basic keys to success, which are delayed gratification, long-term vision and the power of compounding.

After high school, Myron received an athletic scholarship to Jackson State University and of course looking up to him and wanting to be like him, I made my way to Mississippi Valley State University on a baseball scholarship. Our schools were separated by only an hour and a half drive. If you know anything about "The SWAC", the Southwestern Athletic Conference, you know that the schools are known for their awesome homecoming festivities during college football season. Jackson State and Mississippi Valley rank up there at the top of the party list among the historically black colleges and universities. I remember flying down the back roads and highways from Itta Bena, MS to Jackson with hopes of getting onto campus and kicking it with my cousin. It's Homecoming. There are beautiful college girls everywhere. You can hear music coming from all directions. The smell of food is in the air but it wasn't as strong as my anticipation for the night and weekend events. I was ready to party. I shouldn't have been surprised, but I was. Myron had business at hand. He had papers to write and tests to study for. It did not matter what this weekend was or what everyone else was doing. It did not matter that I had traveled an hour and a half to come kick it. First things were first. He welcomed me to go out and have a great time. He even pointed me in the right direction of the best party spots. I flew out just as fast as I had flown in. He studied. A couple of hours into the festivities he shows up. By this time, I've consumed a few adult beverages and am clearly enjoying college life. In about an hour or so he has maybe one drink if any and he's back off to the dorm. There was more work to be done.

That discipline didn't come naturally. He wanted to party just as hard as the rest of us. He enjoyed the same things as most teenagers. He was no different than I, but he had learned some very vital principles. He had a father, day in and day out, teaching him those life lessons and success principles from the time he could crawl. I wasn't afforded the luxury of my father being in my house, teaching me and guiding me to manhood with discipline, dedication and focus. I had to learn the hard way. My road was made very rough by my own choices. It is said that you have to discipline yourself or someone else will. It's much better being done at your own hands rather than your life being controlled by the hands of another.

Myron soon graduates and travels north to the University of Mississippi where he pursues his Master's degree. This time his school, Ole Miss, was an hour and a half away but in a different direction. I traveled north to stay with him for the weekend and could only observe that the discipline and focus had grown stronger. In between the studying, we would go out to eat, talk and do the catching up that cousins do, but it was always back to the task at hand. I was living for the weekend. He was living for his life. He was living to produce the life he wanted to live and be the success that he had determined. He received his Master's Degree in Psychology and eventually earned his Ph.D. in Educational Leadership from the University of Southern Mississippi. Let me add that he is also a graduate of the Harvard Art of Leadership Institute. Dr. Labat (as he is referred to today) was once honored in Ebony magazine as one of the top thirty African American Leaders of the future under the age of thirty. How about that for succeeding in life! His accolades go on and on, with his church and community involvement, as well as his family and entrepreneur endeavors.

Fast-forward a few years to 2005. This is a couple of years after my stint in minor league baseball, working graveyard shift at a casino in Biloxi, MS and substitute teaching at just about every school on the Mississippi Gulf Coast to make ends meet and pay the bills. I was ready to fulfill one of my lifelong dreams of being a teacher and coach. I was twenty-nine years old, I had no degree and I had been out of school for over eight years. It was a fortunate situation. I was hired as a teacher's assistant/assistant coach at my Alma Mater, Pass Christian High School, until I could finish my degree and teacher's certification. Who was the assistant principal? It was none other than Dr. Myron Labat, my very own flesh and blood cousin. I always looked up to him and always wanted to achieve the levels of success that I witnessed first-hand in his life. He was success to me. It wasn't the fake facade that many people put on to appear to be winning at life. He was winning. He was genuinely making sustainable progress in every area of his life. He was not upside down in a fancy house or in debt to his eyebrows from the luxury cars parked in his garage. Dr. Labat was living the American dream; but it was the dream he decided to live long ago. It was decided even before the choices to stay in the dorm room and study during homecoming at Jackson State. It was decided when he decided to listen to his father speak powerful and wise words to him. It was decided when he decided, as a young boy, to take the action steps of those words that lead to success. Dr. Labat moved on from being a high school principal to being the head of the Education Department at the University of Southern Mississippi. He continues to have progressive realizations of worthy causes.

To a certain degree, I knew I could achieve some of the accolades and successes he was receiving. I knew the amount of work and dedication it would take. This was the tale of two cousins virtually cut from the same cloth. We were only different in one way, but that one way is the most powerful and dramatic life-altering way. It was our choices. Those little things that may not seem to be a big deal at the time but are habit forming and destiny shaping in either positive or negative ways. Every choice, no matter how big or small it may seem, is working for you or against you. There is no in between. That choice is going to produce a negative or positive result. The problem is in the fact that at the very moment of our choice we don't realize or believe that something so small will have much of an impact down the road.

At any point, any of us can achieve anything we want. It doesn't matter what we have been through or where we are right now. Your success can start now. A shift can happen right now. The most talented doesn't always finish first. The smartest, fastest, strongest or the better person isn't guaranteed to be the most successful. It's the ones who want it the most and do what it takes to get it. It is those who choose success that will succeed. It bothered me as I sat there in the church hall, that I would never be able to do like my cousin and honor my father. I will never be able to stand up and give a speech on how he made me who I am. I will never be able to give credit to him for helping me become a man and teaching me the lessons of life that I had to learn for the most part on my own; the hard way and intentionally seeking guidance once I became a man. As quick as those feelings of sadness and depression came over me that night, they left. Something went off inside of me. It was the turning point. It was my crossroads. It was time for me to create a Self-directed Shift in my life. I can't be like Myron Jr, the son praising his father. I could be like Myron Sr., the father, being honored by my sons for inspiring them, teaching them, and giving them the wisdom and knowledge that wasn't given to me by my father. I can pass along the keys to success to my three sons as I succeed in my own life. No longer was I sad because I didn't have the life my cousin did coming up. No longer was I jealous because I didn't have a father who did all of those things. I am the father. I will be the father that I didn't have. I will be like my Uncle. I will learn to encourage my sons, develop those strong bonds, teach them those needed life lessons, and be there in their lives. Their road to success starts now. I choose to be a great father. That is my CHOICE.

THE SELF-DIRECTED SHIFT

RICKEY LEWIS

SELF-DIRECTED GROWTH

SELF-DIRECTED EDUCATION

NATURAL PATH OF GROWTH

0 2 4 6 8 10 12 14 16 18 20 22 24 26 28 30 32 34 36 38 40 42 44 46 48 50 60 70 80 90

LIFE SPAN

There is a natural path of growth we are all on throughout our lifetime. That path produces the average results of the average person. We do not have to live our entire life on that path or accept those results in any area of our life. We can choose to shift to a different path and gain different results no matter where you are, no matter your age or your personal situation.

CHAPTER 2

Find a New Path & Create a Shift

"Take up one idea. Make that one idea your life - think of it, dream of it, live on that idea. Let the brain, muscles, nerves, every part of your body, be full of that idea, and just leave every other idea alone. This is the way to success."

-Swami Vivekananda

Something was happening to me. They say that the best way to wake an adult up is to get them learning again. Boy was I learning! I had come alive. Answers to problem were miraculously popping into my head. Problem solving and deciphering the best solutions to the everyday dilemmas of life were becoming child's play. I was even welcoming the challenges of my world. They had become a stimulus, a drug or type of addiction. I had been reading so much that I could quote authors of books and I could recite messages delivered from the speakers of audios and podcasts that I had been listening to. They were giving me answers and helping me solve my own problems. They were creating a thinking machine. This is all coming from a man who had only read one book his entire life outside of a required text for school or work.

Prior to my Self-directed Shift, I didn't really understand personal development and how important it is on one's life. The cobwebs were being cleaned and cleared from this previously empty room I called a head.

One day I was trying to explain something to a friend of mine and he said, "tell it to me like I'm a two-year-old". He just wanted me to give him the information in a clear and simple way. The best way for me to do so and the best way for me to learn is visually, so I created the visual representation of what I have labeled "The Self-Directed Shift". The theory itself is rather simple and doesn't take a rocket scientist to understand. I will try to explain it to you like you're a two-year-old. We are all born naked into this world. We know very little and we learn a lot over the course of our lives. Some things are learned from our parents, from our friends, and from our environment. The knowledge we acquire from year to year produces the results that are in our life. Those results may be material possessions, friendships, money, careers and jobs, our faith, the type of marriage we are involved in, the type of parents we become, and our overall health and physical appearance to name a few. There is a natural progression that we all follow in life. We get better at life as time goes on. Some of it is just maturity. The natural path is paved with trial and error, bumping our head a time or two, and grabbing that hot pan on the stove. Once you've burned your hand pretty good, you become a little wiser and won't do it again. That's the way life works. The longer you live on this earth, the smarter you become. You make better decisions. The results get better. It may not seem like it because your results only increase slightly from year to year. Compare all areas of your life ten years ago to the results now. Think about your first job. Maybe you made minimum wage. Every year since then you have crept up the pay scale. Naturally you will earn more money as time goes on. I think about all of my young romantic relationships. I made mistake after mistake, but with each new relationship I learned and got better. Have you ever heard someone say, "he got old man strength"? Without working out and lifting weights, you will naturally get stronger. Most people -- the average Americans -- follow the path of natural growth. You don't have to do that. I decided not to follow that path. We can look into the future and see where we will be by assessing the slight increases of growth from our past. If that future is not where you want to end up, it's time to start The Self-Directed Shift to a new path of growth. The new path is accelerated and brings forth greater results than what the future yields otherwise. Mommies and daddies can't put you on that path. Your high school and college teachers don't put you on that path. Those roads are on that natural path. The Self-Directed Shift starts with Self. That means you have to decide that you want better out of your life. The divorce rate is high. How about shifting your marriage to the path of higher results by reading great marriage books, seeking counsel before there are problems, and participating in couple's retreats. Are you broke? That's only temporary. You're not poor. Start studying financial principles and learn money management skills. Create the shift in your wallet, pocketbook or purse. Your faith could use a little energizing. It will naturally grow as time goes on, but if you want to be person of great faith, put down the remote control and pick up the bible. The Self-Directed Shift is all about a self-directed education. Pick any area of your life that you would like to have different results and educate yourself on that topic. The shift will happen. Stay on that path by constantly reading, learning and growing. It really doesn't take much to force a shift away from the natural progress and growth to the greater growth and greater results you deserve. Tell yourself that you want better results, believe that you can have them, and start The Self-Directed Shift.

Your life will be a direct reflection of the books you read, the audios you listen to, and the people you associate with. There was my first problem. How could I create a shift in my life if I did not even read? I had to get over it. There was no way around it. If we are truly going to change something in our lives, we are going to have to change something in our lives. I was going to have to pick up a book and actually read it. My whole life, I've heard that the answers to life's questions were in books. You could say that I wasn't trying to answer any of those questions.

Have you read a book lately? How about one that can impact your life in a way no other words have. Sure, we read newspapers, celebrity gossip columns, and magazines. What about a book designed to help you grow and develop principles and character within yourself? How about developing discipline?

Follow the trail. I found a pattern that made itself evident as I started my journey of a self-directed shift. I've been reading books and listening to world-class authors, speakers and motivators. Each one of those persons references other world-class authors, speakers and motivators. Iron sharpens iron. They point you in a direction that they have already traveled. You only need to follow. It is like an intricate web of knowledge waiting for you to get trapped in ... like a small insect. Maybe it's like being trapped in a maze that you can never leave. Once you start reading and learning from great people and great materials, you can't stop. Right now I am reading author John C. Maxwell's book *"The 15 Invaluable Laws of Growth"*. He is one of the top personal development experts in the world and he has referenced a couple of dozen other authors just halfway through this book. Some of those authors I know and have read their works. They themselves have referenced Maxwell. I've stated before that facts change but principles are forever. Each author writes on principles, which may be between the lines of their thoughts and stories. Each one has a unique way of getting those principles across to the readers. I've been highlighting authors and books mentioned in this book because I am eager to follow the path that John C. Maxwell has traveled. It's like Hansel and Gretal walking through the woods on a path, picking up gumdrops to find their way home; but you will never get home. Attaining knowledge is not a destination. It is a journey. Change is growing in every area of your life and you should always be growing. One of my first mentors in life used to say, " You're not grown until you're in the graveyard". You should be growing your whole life. There should be some intentional change and growth taking place every day. All you have to do is start with one book or audio from a world-class leader in personal development and follow the trail. They will lead you to the next person and to the next. You just have to start somewhere. Jump into that web. Get yourself lost in the maze of knowledge and develop your wisdom. There are some world-class authors and speakers that have changed my life and the results that my family and I see. We CHOOSE to grow.

Try reading *"The Slight Edge"* by Jeff Olson. It's an awesome book. There is a slight edge working in your life right now and you may not even know it. It is either working for you or against you. At least look it up. Take an action step and follow my lead. You have nothing else better to do with your life than to grow. You have already started your Self-directed Shift because you are reading this book. By the time you are finished, you will be ready for more. The hunger and thirst will be ever so present and I will not disappoint with the direction to the next gumdrop. Your list of authors and world-class speakers will grow. You will only have to take the next step on your path, which is outside of the normal growth and on the Self-directed Shift.

It doesn't matter how young or how old you are to start reading. I started reading and my whole world changed. The world I knew for thirty plus years. I have experienced what Stephen Covey calls a paradigm shift. My view and outlook on life are no longer the same. I can see a better way, a more effective way of life. My vision has shifted from seeing the world in a new light. My new vision leads me to a better belief system, which leads me to better actions. Those actions are leading to the best results of my life.

I became so excited to see my kindergartener read a book for the first time last night. Reading for the first time, his world has changed. Sure, the book was about a cat chasing a rat that sat by a hat, but he is putting letters together to make words that are making sentences. His process of understanding is growing. A book is a powerful thing, especially a good book.

I started reading "The Magic of Thinking Big" last night with my eight-year-old because I wanted to educate him on the power of belief. One of my eighteen-year-old students believes that she is too young to do anything about her life. I almost flipped out, but I had to think. Would I have "received" that type of information at eighteen that I am trying to teach this generation? I don't know, but I wish someone would have tried to give me this knowledge back then. She stated that all she knows to do is to go to school.

I talked with a co-worker last night as he left his night class in pursuit of his Master's degree. We both agreed that the benefit of most degrees is not always directly related to being educated. I have learned more in the last few years from my self-directed education than in all of my years sitting at a desk in high school or an institute of higher learning. By no means am I trying to devalue formal education. It has its place and purpose in our path to success. My learning stems from opening books that have propelled my growth and progress past the normal maturing and learning curve of life. When was the last time you had a growth spurt in your education? You may not remember the last time, but the next time is starting right now. You've started reading. Now you just have to keep going to the next page, to the next chapter and to the next book. Your Self-directed Shift is emerging.

Hardly do I ever recommend movies, especially fictional movies. The fact is that I have not been watching very many movies lately. The television has become less of a necessity than it has ever been in my life. My wife and I have elected to eliminate the cable television from our lives. For one, the financial cost of rising cable bills is an area we could cut in an attempt to reduce our debts and increase our wealth. Many of our friends and family think of it as odd or unusual not to have some type of cable programming. Secondly, the cost of the subliminal messaging through commercials and other programs on the minds of our children and us as well is too great to chance.

With that being said I would suggest that you watch the movie *Phenomenon* starring John Travolta. I've seen this movie before but this time watching it, I caught it in a different light. I related to this character. He was an average guy in a small town that started doing some extraordinary things. He started problem-solving, coming up with great ideas, and helping others in ways he had not before. In no way do I compare myself to the genius of his character, and I am not saying that I am doing extraordinary things. I just understood the process of what was happening in his life. Again, the best way to wake up an adult is to get them learning again. I have been awakened by all of the possibilities that exist out there in the world. You too can experience this awakening and enlightenment through the power of reading. Travolta's character, George Malley, started reading four to five books a day. And the wheels in his brain just kept spinning. The more he reads, the more he learns. The more he learns, the more problems he solves. Our value lies in our ability to solve problems. If you want to increase your value as a human being to our society or to your family or job, start solving more problems. Dr. Myles Monroe states that our value is based on the level of problems we solve. Take any company or organization. The person with the highest value is usually the one who solves the biggest problems, or the most problems. In turn, they usually command the higher wage. I've been reading more than I have ever read before. Subsequently I am now learning more than I have ever learned in my entire life. Today we must all solve problems whether it is in our marriages, on our jobs, or in our community organizations. Why not prepare and arm ourselves with information and knowledge? Why don't we wake up and start learning? Why not create a shift in our thinking? It all starts with transformational reading.

I have been asked to speak to the youth on goal setting and achievement, and to large congregations on modeling through faith. I've been giving welcome speeches at family reunions for families I don't even belong to. I've been truly blessed and I know that God is using me for His purpose as I discover my own.

I'm not special. I don't have big fancy degrees from the best schools around the country. I'm just a Mississippi boy who had big dreams of having a life better than the one I was living. Many look at me today and are baffled by my recent actions and my passion for personal development. The fact is that a few years ago no one would have asked me for marriage advice. No way would any sane person ask me to speak to a group on leadership principles, and parents weren't calling me for help in getting through to their troubled teen.

I read. I apply the information in my life, and I share what I have learned with the world. Studying successful people is a must. Studying success principles is without a doubt the most impactful element in my success process. This isn't about me. It's about you. It's about you getting the results you want and need in your life by doing some of the things I have done and are suggesting to you.

My wife and I took a small weekend vacation to visit some of her college friends, and attend a wedding of one of her sorority sisters of Delta Sigma Theta, Inc. It was a beautiful wedding and a beautiful weekend being shared with old friends of hers and new friends of mine. My journey in growth has taken me into some unfamiliar places; strange and outside of the realm of what I have been used to. On Friday night we had a wonderful dinner prepared by our host; we played games, and reminisced over old school music played on our cell phones. Breakfast was served the next morning and we discussed life, success and the secrets that escape so many of our peers. How blessed my wife and I were to be engaging in meaningful and intellectual conversations with like-minded people, educators and entrepreneurs.

We had some time to kill before the wedding so the women decided to go do a little shopping. There was nothing odd about that. That's what women do, don't they? What was strange or odd is what us men did. We went to a Books-a-Million bookstore, got coffee, and discussed authors such as John Maxwell, Dave Ramsey and Michael Gerber, author of "The E-Myth Revisited". I'm 6'2" tall and my friend is a 6'9" former basketball star at the University of Southern Mississippi. We should have been somewhere shooting some hoops. Well that would have been something inside of normal for me a few years ago. Now there is, in his words, a new normal. That is Purposefully growing, learning, and developing yourself for a more successful and productive life. With any of the friends I grew up with, this would not have happened. We would not have intentionally gone to a bookstore for leisure. We would have gone to the basketball court, rode around town listening to the latest music, had a barbecue, or just found a tree to sit and drink beers under. The conversation wouldn't have been about intentionality, awareness and reflection. It would have been about Sean Payton, Michael Vick, and who had the best team in the NFC or SEC. Don't get me wrong. Being a former professional athlete, I enjoy the sports conversations; but they do little to enhance my life. I'd rather talk about Earl Nightingale's thoughts on the secrets of success versus talking about Earl Campbell's NFL rushing yards in 1978. All that mattered before doesn't matter now if it is not about securing my family, future and becoming the best person that I can be.

We have to create a new normal. We have to do things differently to get different results. A bookstore is a great place to read! That day I picked up "The 15 Invaluable Laws of Growth" by John C. Maxwell. He's at the top of many lists on leadership and personal development. I couldn't put it down. I walked out that day with a new gold nugget to add to my collection.

Here is a lesson I learned from Earl Nightingale, author of "Lead the Field". Our level of Success in life is determined by the extent of our knowledge of the language we speak. How good is your vocabulary? You may look very nice. You may be packaged very well on the outside. But when you open your mouth there is no hiding where you fit on the social pyramid. In schools, students excel in all different subject areas like math, science, and the arts; but those who consistently make the highest grades overall and excel to the top of the class are those who excel in vocabulary. I didn't make great grades in school, but I was really good in math and science. I was excellent in art and physical education was a no-brainer. I never read very well and couldn't spell to save my life. To this day, I still struggle with spelling. I stayed away from reading and hated vocabulary during my youth.

When my oldest son Landon was eight years old, he had a vocabulary that exceeded the one I had when I was eighteen. I remember years ago listening to his young speech as he used words that were well beyond the scope of most of the kids his age. I was proud of the fact that I had produced such an intelligent offspring. Contrary to what many may believe, he was not simply a product of good genes. His mother was and is a highly intellectual being; but Landon's I.Q. and intelligence is much more the result of his mother and me reading to him from birth ... and subsequently, him becoming a voracious reader. He loves to read; so his vocabulary expands. The expansion of each person's vocabulary correlates with the expansion of their personal knowledge, I.Q., aptitude, and intelligence. All of these things increase one's value and potential to manifest success in any area of their life. Hats off to my wife, the Queen of the Library, a voracious reader herself. She pushes that initiative in our house. If you say a word that our children don't know, they will promptly ask, "What does that mean?" Before you can answer they would have taken a guess. Many people don't take the time to learn their own language. Learning one word actually gains you several other words because of how words are connected and interwoven in our language.

Our spoken language greatly influences the extent of our knowledge. The two go hand in hand. Knowledge will lead us to our success. We really need to read more and study our language. I use to get frustrated when I couldn't express myself because of the lack of words in my vocabulary bank. I know that there are words that can help me effectively communicate my thoughts. I am constantly working on my vocabulary, and I have committed to reading every day. I use the dictionary to locate and learn new words to use in place of my RUDIMENTARY vocabulary. Early one morning my wife asked Landon to spell "cirrus". I drew a blank, but seconds later he rattled off the letters C-I-R-R-U-S and gave its reference to a type of cloud. The dictionary is not a bad place to start reading and learning. Pick one up today and thumb through the pages. You could add a few more words to your vocabulary, increase your knowledge, and move further towards your success.

CHAPTER 3

Belief and Thinking

"Those who believe they can move mountains, do. Those who believe they can't, cannot. Belief triggers the power to do."

-David J. Schwartz

Creating a Self-directed Shift is going to have to start with a shift in your thinking. It will have to start with your mind first. We need new ways of thinking and new levels of processing information in our heads. *"You see, we must first win the battle in our minds before we can even begin to see action. Taking on change without first getting your thoughts in line is like running out on the battlefield with a sword and armor without taking training classes on martial arts and proper equipment use. The odds are against you."* -Crystal Scretching, *Pass the Mustard Seed*

Many years ago I was drafted by a Major League baseball team and started my six-year career as a professional athlete. I quickly realized that the journey to make it to "The Show", out of the Minors and into the Majors would be a hard task. Today with my studies, I realize that my chances of ever making it back then were Slim to None because of my thinking and belief system. Thinking is the backbone to all success. My physical ability and athleticism had nothing to do with my success or failure. It was my thinking.

It may be your thinking and processing skills that may be holding you back. From the neck down we are all worth minimum wage. It is from the neck up where we create our worth. Yes, we can create our worth. We are all born with different aptitudes and brain functioning capabilities, but we are all able to deliberately increase the output of our minds. It takes intentional working of your mental muscles by reading empowering books and applying principles for growth. If I had my youth and that twenty-one year old body with the brainpower and mental strength that I have gained today, the sky would have been the limit. We all have heard of the phrase " If I only knew then what I know now". I'm not just talking about the knowledge. That is on the path of natural growth. I'm talking about intentionally increasing your functioning capability. There is a difference.

I often live in Fantasy Land and have to snap myself out of it from time to time. I imagine a back-to-the future scenario where today's me goes back and hands the 1998 version of myself a copy of David J. Schwartz, "*The Magic of Thinking Big*". I realize we can't change the past, but we can predict and control most of the outcomes of our future by changing the way we think today. Some of the most influential authors, speakers, and teachers of life lessons use the power of our minds as the basis for success in any field. Napolean Hill wrote *"Think and Grow Rich"*. John C. Maxwell's *"Thinking for A Change"* can catapult your life forward. James Allen wrote *"As a Man Thinketh"*, a great illustration on how powerful our mind and thoughts are. I could go on and on about the greats through history who knew the power of thought. You can change your life by controlling the thoughts you think to produce the results you want. Ralph Waldo Emerson said, *"Great men are those who see that thoughts rule the world."* The Self-directed shift is a shift in your thinking. It is educating your mind into a change. The first step is to accept the fact that you need a shift in some area of your life. Work on your thoughts. Work on training your brain. We need to change our paradigm. How do we change our thought process? We change the information we are putting into our heads. We read life changing books with empowering information. Then we put our brains to work by controlling ourselves into new actions. Think big and think change.

A paradigm shift is a fundamental change in an approach or in our underlying assumptions. Our paradigm is the way we assume things are. It is what we believe is truth based on our backgrounds, teachings, environmental influences and our experiences. Your paradigm is essentially a description of you projected onto the world and into every situation. Stephen R. Covey explains it this way in his book " The 7 Habits of Highly Effective People". He was sitting in the subway when a man and his three sons came in. The boys were out of control running around and bothering people. The man sat there in a daze saying nothing. Finally Mr. Covey said to the man, "Can you please get your kids under control!" The man sat up and said apologetically, " I guess I should. You see we just left the hospital an hour ago and their mother just died. They don't know how to react and I don't either." Stephen Covey had a paradigm shift because he was given new information.

Imagine if everyone in that subway knew that information. How many would've changed the way they felt and reacted. How you see affects how you feel and how you react. I have had a complete paradigm shift in my life. I see a lot of situations differently now because of the new information I am receiving. It is scary to think that I have had a curtain in front of my eyes for so long. I used to get upset because I couldn't help others see what I was seeing. Their perception is their reality. It doesn't mean that it is the truth. It's the truth to them. Our paradigms are changing all the time. You probably looked at the world differently when you became a parent or when you were made the manager or shift-leader at your job. The best way to change a person's behavior is to change a person's paradigm. Change the information that they are receiving. I forced life-changing information into my head. My mental vision cleared up and I regained a 20/20 perception. The cataracts are gone! I see people differently now. I see my future differently now. My purpose in life is being revealed because of a paradigm shift. My self-directed education has proven to show more gains than my formal education and college degree. You have to believe that there is a better way out there. You have to believe that you can improve in every area of your life. Welcome new information and prepare for your shift in thinking.

Perspective has a lot to do with the interpretation of events. I know that you are familiar with the saying "on the outside looking in". Many people can look at the same event or situation and there ends up being several different interpretations of what happened, why it happened and whose fault it was. Each person is sure (100%) that their view or opinion is right. Heck, they saw it with their own eyes. The problem is that all of our eyes are looking at the same thing, but the view to which we see can be totally different than a person just five feet away. D'Urso, my friend who is an automobile painter, has painted vehicles that change or flip colors. That's nothing new, but think about this. I can put three people in three different places looking at a car that he's painted and all three would say that it is a different color. One would swear that it is blue; one would say purple; and the other would bet his life that it's green. Each would be correct. As my brother Zak would say " to a certain degree". As we make judgments, speak on truths and argue our points, we need to be aware of other viewpoints and perspectives. We must first understand others' perspective. Walk in his shoes before you judge. Don't just think she's crazy because she has different political views than you. Try to understand why people think the way they do. It is their view, their perspective or vantage point. The world would be so much better if we tried to understand what others are seeing and why they think the way they do, instead of judging the validity of what they believe. I was told this a long time ago. Don't believe anything you hear and only half of what you see. Well, you can believe what you hear from me and seeing is all about perspective. Ask David Copperfield.

Where is it? Is it taped to your bathroom mirror, in the pocket of your daily planner, or tucked in your bible near your favorite scripture? Maybe it's still in your head or you just haven't put it together yet. Have you not built the courage to write it out? What are you waiting on! I'm talking about your bucket list.

At some point, you must decide that there are some things that are already inside of you that you will accomplish. Those things have been forming inside of us since we were young. Some have just been formed and they all are very important. There is no reason that all of us shouldn't be working on that list and crossing those tasks off one by one. First it must be formed, and it should be in our face where we can see it everyday. You have to develop belief. This is where most of us get stuck. Our belief systems are shot. Do you believe you can accomplish this task? Try connecting your belief to feelings. Believe it as if you have already done it. Imagine what it feels like to be sitting in Paris under the bright city lights. Smell the foods and see the people enjoying them in the new restaurant you've just opened. What does the sand feel like between your toes as you walk down the beaches in Maui? Do you see the crystal clear waters and hear the calming waves roll onto the shore? What does the sun feel like on your face? Thoughts become things when there is belief that is connected to feelings. Work on your belief. Every day you should be working on your belief. It doesn't have to just be in accomplishing your bucket list. Work on your belief in everything and anything being possible.

The Self-directed Shift that you are creating is attached to the greatest system known to man. It is your very own belief system. It is a beacon, a lighthouse or an enormous bright blinking sign pointing you in the direction you either want to go or don't. Whatever you believe is your truth. The man who thinks he can and the man who thinks he can't are both right. Simply put, beliefs guide you. Increase your beliefs and you increase your actions. That belief will make you work harder. It will force your foot to step forward.

Just about everything that you can think of, has been done by someone else so you can do it as well. If it is so rare that no one has accomplished it yet, so what. You'll be the first. Believe that. Feel that! I know it's hard and has been a long journey, but see yourself walking across that stage shaking hands with the Dean as he hands you that diploma. You better keep believing it. Hear those high heels tapping that wooden floor as you stroll across with a big Kool-Aid smile. Believe that you will debt free. Can you see yourself writing that last check to the mortgage company? Have you imagined walking down that aisle? Of course you've done that, but do you believe it? Can you feel your father clutching your arm as your legs tremble and tears run down your cheek? You will get that job. Believe it. See yourself in that position doing all of the duties of the job. What does it feel like? Believe in yourself. Believe that you can do anything, have anything, and be anything. Connect it all to feelings because those feeling manifest themselves into real life tangible things.

Anything you want and desire can be yours no matter how big or small. There is a group of people walking this earth who have harnessed the power that produces the life that they want. Only about five percent of the people in this world earn ninety-five percent of the money. They are not smarter, luckier, or even been chosen to accumulate all of the wealth in the world. They have found the secret, which has been utilized throughout time. The secret is the law of attraction. We attract everything we have in our lives. We become everything we think about. We can have what we can visualize. It all starts with the way we think and our thoughts. Thoughts become things. If you can harness the power of visualization, you can determine what your life will look like.

Attraction works with positive and negative outcomes. Most people think mostly about the things they don't want and that's what they attract. Think about how many times you have said, " I don't want be late", that thought takes over your mind and you end up being late. You attracted that. If you tell yourself that you're going to get sick or you constantly say that you don't want to be sick, you will attract sickness. If you constantly complain about the type of people you don't want in your life, that's who shows up. If you don't want your son dating someone of a different race, same sex, financially challenged, too young or too old, guess who's coming to dinner!

Start focusing on the thing you want, what you do have, and show gratitude for all that God has given you. It will attract more. The law of attraction responds to your thoughts whether they are good or bad. All of the books I have been reading on personal development, changing your life, and leadership all lead back to one central focus. That focus is your thoughts. The way we think, and the power that the mind has to control our destiny. We determine what our lives will look like. It all may sound a bit far-fetched, but I assure you that it is true. In the process of changing the way I think about things, I've started getting better results out of life. Not just material things, but better relationships, health and overall good feelings that lead to happiness and joy. Command positive things and eliminate all negative thoughts. The law of attraction is always working no matter how much you believe in it, understand it or don't care about it. If you think positively, you will attract positive things and people. Negative people are always having negative experiences and attracting more negative people.

I give you this warning. Choose your thoughts carefully. Be careful what you ask for and think about, you just may get it. Look around you right now. Everything in your life good or bad, you attracted it. A big part of this secret is accepting the fact that you attracted those bad things that happened in your life as well as the good. Once you've mastered that, you can start attracting all of the things you want. Read "The Secret" by Rhonda Byrne, or watch the documentary. It may change your life by changing the way you think about what you are attracting.

She always looks at the glass as half empty. She's a good friend that I admire for her many qualities, but I often get perturbed by her attitude. She takes offense to me calling her negative. She looks at it as being realistic. It's a pessimistic attitude towards life. Do you have friends like that? Are you that type of person? Is the glass half full or half empty? It's her defense mechanism.

The more I read, learn, and apply the principles of positive attitudes, positive thoughts, and the magic of thinking big, I realize what her true downfall is. I understand why a person of her caliber with good character and integrity is not accomplishing the great things that she is capable of. If the odds are stacked against her, she's not going that way. She's not going to take that risk. Life has dealt her some tough blows, but it has done the same for many others who refuse to allow it to affect their outlook on the future. I tried to explain to her that negative things are going to happen in our lives. We can't prevent it all, but we can eliminate a lot of it from happening with the power of our positive thoughts. If we think positive it will lead to positive actions and those actions will lead to positive results.

If you don't believe you can do something, you're not going to take the necessary steps to lead to positive results. That's when you say, "I knew I couldn't do that" or "I told you that it wouldn't work for me". The person who thinks they can and the person who thinks they can't are both right. It all starts with thought. We have to eliminate the negative thoughts. Attitude is everything in life. It's belief that's the magic formula that separates equally talented people from those who achieve and those who don't. I was not the most talented on my high school baseball team. I was not the best pitcher from my hometown. I could name five guys from my little small town who were physically better than me. No, I was not lucky. I thought differently. I didn't look at the odds of me being a professional baseball player as a negative thing. I looked at it as a positive possibility. Even one in a million, means you have a chance! If your thoughts don't begin to change, then your results won't.

My friend will never know the power of positive thoughts. She is trapped inside of that negative glass. Until she can force herself out of the realm of "being real", eliminating all negative thought, building on her positive attitude, and believing and knowing she can accomplish all that her heart desires, she will continue to receive the negative outcomes that she focuses on. I have seen the results of focusing on the positive and eliminating all of the negative. It's almost like magic! If you fill your brain with positive, there will be no room for negative.

CHAPTER 4

Happiness, Feelings & Emotions

"Happiness is not achieved by the conscious pursuit of happiness; it is generally the by-product of other activities."

-Aldous Huxley

Most people in this world are not happy; yet we all pursue happiness. Raise your hand if you are truly happy in just about every area of your life. The average American wishes they had another job or are not doing what they think would make them happy as a career. Very few are working in an area that they intentionally chose. You may be working somewhere and don't really know how you ended up there. Maybe you just floated through life and this is where the tide took you. That is just one area of your life.

We may not really know how to define happy, but we know it when we see it. It is recognizable through our feelings. We are very poor at knowing what truly makes us happy and others often miss the mark of making us happy, we are always giving people the power in dictating our happiness. Our expectations of others to make us happy fails and we become angry or upset at them as if it is their responsibility. It's not. Why is it that we chase one thing after another? Why do we go from relationship to relationship? We are searching for happiness. We are searching for that one job, the one thing or that one person to make us happy. It doesn't happen. Happiness is a by-product of other things, but we pursue it directly. So many people in this world are not really pursuing happiness. They are pursuing pleasure. Pleasure is not fulfilling. It is just a stimulant. As you pursue these pleasures, they demand more and more of that stimulant. That's where addiction and obsessions begin. Passion brings us closer to happiness. Passion fires us up! It is a feeling that burns inside of us. It is a driving force to our destinations in life that are guided by those beliefs we talked about earlier. We need these emotions that can lead us to our purpose in life, which we will discuss later. First, let's talk about happiness and emotions.

Where are you on a scale of one to ten when it comes to happiness? Whatever number you have conjured up in the back of your mind is probably off by a point or two. We become comfortable in our discomfort. Human beings are really good at adjusting to survive. Most of that is from a mental/emotional state. We tell ourselves that we are okay when we really are not and that subsequently makes things okay. We are good at tricking our brains into believing we really didn't want that thing that we truly desired but fell short on attaining it. It is our compensation mechanism. That is just a mental trick. How about taking it a step further!

We are ready to create a Self-directed Shift in our happiness. It's time to focus on that. Who doesn't want to be happy? There are many things that you can do and are going to have to intentionally work on to create a significant and sustainable shift in the area of true happiness in your life.

"Is there something right now in your life that you love to do? There are things that each of us knows in our heart that we love to do. There are all these facets of life that you can find and that you can really genuinely love. Maybe you love doing your makeup. Maybe you love doing your sister's hair. It can be something so simple, right. Now for me, when I was eight years old, I didn't love to run. I loved to spend time with my older sister and my day. A few years later I realized that running was something I loved. It gave me something to look forward to everyday and a time to think about my life, think about where I was or spend time with my sister. And that's what got me to love running. It's not just running. It can be anything. I maybe would have found my place somewhere else but at that time running is what served that purpose for me. I think that it's important that when you are young, when you are in middle school or high school, you start to search for that thing that you truly love because I can easily name a hundred things I don't love to do. I don't love to go swimming. I don't love to make my bed. I don't love to do a thousand things every single day but I do have a couple of things I live for. That is tough. The younger you are when you figure that out, it can be more difficult. When I was in the eight grade, I really started to love what I was doing which

brings me to my next point. You got to make sure that you are surrounded by people who love that you have found what you love to do. There's going to be a day where each one of you find something you're actually passionate about and one of the difficult things is to find support."

Cory McGee, (Professional Track Athlete Sponsored by New Balance)

Chris Brady, leadership author and speaker, states that the only way to be happy is to give happy. When we feel unhappy, depressed, down or have been robbed of that feeling, we should serve others. Make others happy and take the focus off of you. Give happiness to others. That by-product of happiness will boomerang back to us almost as a reward for doing the right things. When I feel down or depressed, I act as if someone else is feeling that same way. It may be a friend, co-worker or family member. I show them love, compassion and care. No matter how they were really feeling, my attention to them uplifts and warms their heart. The feelings of joy that they exude, replicates inside of me. It is just like a boomerang. If you throw happiness out there into the world, it has no choice but to come back.

How will you find your "happy" today? Every day, something, an event or someone will try to steal your joy. There's always something that seems to want to destroy the little hope that we rise with every morning. People in our lives are great at sucking the life from underneath our fingertips. Some are intentional, but many drain and draw from us without knowing what they do. Those are the naturally pessimistic people who can't see or don't want to see the hope in your eyes. Subconsciously they need company in the misery and gloom that burdens their soul. To find your happiness, you will need to steer clear of certain people because they will not allow you to find it. They may be the ones hiding it from you. It may be your mother, sister, brother or best friend. Evaluate your relationships and acquaintances. If they aren't lifting you up, pushing forward or believing in your vision, limit the time you give them. Love them where they are, but don't allow yourself to be brought to their level. Some people have been surrounded by the negative so long and have not enjoyed the true happiness of life. Being negative is normal to them. It may be as simple as "this job sucks", "today's a horrible day", or "why bother". No matter how large or small the negativity is, find your "happy" by finding yourself distant from negative people. Find your "happy" by only sharing your time with positive people.

It is very possible that Monday is the most hated day of the week. This day robs so many of us of our happiness. This is the day the Lord has made. It's no different than any other. So, I understand that now. I haven't always. We can't afford to give away our happiness.

Here's the cure for the Monday blues on any job. This is for those who may not be working in your field of purpose, because when you are, every day is the same. It's a wonderful day to be doing what you were called to do and love. People drag in with a terrible attitude and the day is doomed from the start. They're sad that the weekend is over. Maybe their football team lost a big game on Sunday or maybe they won, but they spent all of their energy yelling at the television screen to help them win. No matter what the case, a majority of people feel down on Mondays. Spirits are at an all-time low on this first day of the workweek. Do you just accept it as just that? Have you submitted to Mondays being a drag? They don't have to be. Our thoughts, our thinking and our feelings are the sources of our happiness. Decide that you want your Mondays to be just like Fridays. I was tired of going through the day as if there was a dark cloud looming over my head. Here is what I did.

I would go to bed Sunday night thinking that tomorrow will be a great day. I would get up Monday morning and pick out a nice suit to wear. We are not required to wear suits at my job. If you are required to wear a suit to your job, pick your favorite one. Ladies, grab the nicest dress or set of work clothes that you have hanging in the closet. Do your hair especially nice. Wear your favorite fragrance. Even put on your lucky underwear. It's hard to feel bad when you look good. Use Monday as the day you dress your best. Make Monday's outfit almost over the top. Be different than normal (in a good way). Walk a little bit faster. Put some pep in your step. It emits confidence to others. All day long people will compliment you.

Do you know how hard it is to feel bad if people are constantly saying how nice you look?! Do you think you will drag through the day if every half hour someone says, "that sure is a pretty dress"? A compliment on that new perfume or cologne will draw a smile on your face. Give as many compliments away to others as you can. They will return the favor and you will feel great. Remember to give happy. Give as much as you can without being over the top, fake or phony. Even if they only say thank you and smile, it will boomerang and fill you with joy. When someone asks, "How do you feel?" reply with, " I feel great! ". You will begin to feel great. The snowball effect will take place. You don't have to do what I did, but you do need to find your cure. We never have to accept the things we don't want. We have a choice. We decide what our world looks like, inside and out. Make Monday a great day.

Happiness is just one emotion, but it is the one we seek the most. There are actually hundreds you could name by definition but in some shape, form, or fashion they can be broken down to fit into about twelve. All of them point us to or drive us away from happiness. If we can learn to control them, we can control or destiny. Your emotions are one of the biggest driving forces of your life. It is quite possible that your emotional state creates all of your results. We study principles, techniques and procedures to do the right things in life. There are laws set and established in the universe that can give you your every desire and need, yet we can't seem to follow them. It is because of emotion. When emotions take over, your rational thinking goes out of the door. We have emotional eating, emotional behaviors and worst of all emotional thinking. We have to learn to tap into the emotion and use it to our advantage. Most people have no control over their emotions because they don't understand that they do have control over their emotions. They just have not harnessed the power. Between stimulus and response is choice. Decision is the greatest power in this world. I can give you the answer to a problem you are having in your life. I'm not talking about an opinion or something I think will work. I'm talking about an actual fact or principle that will solve your situation. For example: You have to lose weight. Answer: Burn more calories than you take in and stabilize your blood sugar by eating a fat, carb, and protein at every meal. Anyone in the world who does that will lose weight. Problem: You can't save any money. Answer: Never spend over 75% of what you make net, control your expenses, and in four years you will have one year's salary saved. The answers to all of your problems are out there in black and white. You have to decide and just do what it is to make it happen. We make excuses why we don't achieve or solve our problems. Many excuses may have validity, but if you get the right emotions working on your side, you can do anything and you won't make excuses. You become creative and resourceful in getting to the answer. Emotions control your decisions and those decisions create your destiny. Explore the emotions that are controlling your life. Explore what makes you tick.

Use your emotions to drive you to succeed. Each one of us is different. You may be driven by love when others are driven by fear. Anger may be a problem. This emotion causes many to destroy positive work and positive steps forward that they have taken in life. As a coach, I see many young people on the football field or basketball court who lose their whole game because they lose their cool. They lose emotional control. It may be a bad call by a referee or umpire. It may be a mistake on their part and the emotion takes over. Often we have to pull players out of the game so that they can get themselves together. It's so that they can regain emotional control.

I was in spring training with the Milwaukee Brewers in Phoenix, Arizona. At the end of a long, grinding day, my pitching coach told me that the head coordinator of the minor league wanted to see me. I thought nothing of it. I walked to his office with a smile on my face, but as I got close to the door there was a line of a few guys and one looked as if he had been crying. He was physically upset. I knew then what it was. It was cutting day. My throat swelled up, muscles got tight and my stomach turned. Finally it was my turn to face the Grim Reaper. This may have been one of the most traumatic events of my life. There were two gentlemen who called me in and sat across from me at a desk. They started talking and the whole scene was so surreal to me. They were stealing my happiness. They were destroying my dream. They may as well have been stabbing me with a knife. That's what it felt like. I've never felt a pain like that from words my entire life. They weren't even screaming. It was a monotone speech that probably had been said by those two at least ten times that day. My plane ticket to fly back to Gulfport, Mississippi was right there on the desk and the plane was scheduled to leave in just about three hours.

Just about every gut-wrenching emotion you can think of was swirling around inside of me. They were abusing me. What they were saying, the words and the tone were totally different from how I was taking them. I'm looking into their eyes and I was ready to snap. I wanted to jump across that desk and hurt them just as bad as they were hurting me. I had had this dream since I was seven years old. I had been on this path for twenty plus years and they were kicking me off of it. I felt like Ralphie in "A Christmas Story" when Santa told him that he would shoot his eye out and then pushed him down the slide. I at least wanted to use some choice words and curse the ground that these two walked on. My emotions were saying let them have it. I took a step closer to the desk, opened my mouth and stuck out my hand. The only words that should have and did come out of my mouth were words of gratitude for having given me an opportunity in the first place. No one could believe that they released me. My friends and teammates thought I was joking. Oh how I wish I were. I wanted to cry. First from the being released just moments earlier, then having to face my peers and knowing I had to face family, friends and those who never believed I would make it anyway, back in Mississippi. I was an emotional wreck. I couldn't even call anyone. I didn't even want to get on the plane. I contemplated just staying out in Arizona for a while to figure my next step. The more time that passed, the more I wished I would've left that office with a blaze of glory that would have let them know just how tough I was and exactly what I thought about these two (insert expletive). They really were okay guys doing their jobs. I was a guy on the brink of losing it. I was a guy about to lose emotional control.

About a month or so later, an independent league baseball team signed me. I traveled to Madison, Wisconsin where my dream continued and my path, which was now on a side street, was still moving forward. After that short season and me doing fairly well, I traveled to Tampa, Florida because I had heard of an open try-out for the Tampa Bay Devil Rays. I was hopeful that I could make the cut and get an invitation to spring training until I arrived and saw almost three hundred participants. Two hundred were pitchers like me. Putting the situation aside, I took the opportunity to do my best. Tony Saunders, a scout for the Rays and one time major league pitcher, took notice and came over to talk with me. I was floored because this was the same Tony Saunders whom I had watched clip after clip of his arm snapping in half during the delivery of a pitch in a Major League game. He was excited about what I could bring to the organization and I was somewhat pleased with his conversation, but the chances of me getting signed were slim. I remember telling myself that no one was getting signed out of here. This is all a media stunt for public relations; but if anyone did, it would be me.

Weeks go by and I get an email from a friend in Wisconsin telling me congratulations on being signed by Tampa Bay. The same day I get a phone call from some friends who live in Tampa. They said that it was in the newspaper that the Devil Rays signed three guys out of that camp. I immediately called the front office of the organization and confirmed that they were sending me a contract in the mail and gave me a reporting date for spring training.

Now, why would I tell you this story? During spring training that year I ran across Tony Saunders. Come to find out, I was the first person he had signed as a scout. He couldn't believe that the Brewers had released me so soon. My numbers weren't terrible. I wasn't old. I had an athletic frame with great potential and good velocity on my fastball. He thought that there probably was an underlying issue. Maybe I was a hot head with a temper, un-coachable, not disciplined or a cancer in the clubhouse. He had to do some investigation. He called the same two guys from Milwaukee who had released me that day in the office. He told me that they had nothing but good things to say about me. It was unfortunate that they had to release me when they did. From a talent and potential aspect, there were others who should have been released besides myself but those players had more of a financial investment tied to their status with the organization.

Imagine what the conversation may have been like if I would have exploded that day. That bridge would have been burned. Tampa would have never signed me and I would have never known why. Your emotional control will dictate where you can and where you will go in life. It is not always easy. Sometimes they get the best of us and we have to pay the consequences of losing control. On your path and Self-directed Shift, you must learn to recognize these feelings inside of you and act accordingly to the results you want to have.

Let me tell you about the time I almost lost it all. This is one of the worst periods of my life. I didn't hold it together. My emotional control was tested and a 5'9" 160lb teenage boy who thought he was 6'5" 250lbs pushed me to the limit. He had his own emotional issues. He was the starting quarterback on our football team during a pretty rough season of losing. The season was unraveling and the morale of the team and coaching staff was in the dump.

The young man became enraged at the treatment of some of the players, particularly his younger brother, because of their lack of effort in some of our tackling drills. When I grew up, football was a man's sport. It was hard nose and grueling both physically and mentally. Coaches got in your face, grabbed you by the ego and whipped you into shape. We stood up and rose to the occasion. In my opinion, the new generation of young athletes is entitled and sensitive. They can't handle an in-your-face approach. I was definitely in his face. I expected him to back down but he didn't. He raised his volume level to a ten. I felt my control rapidly slipping away. I raised my level to twelve. I did and said things that I shouldn't have said to a teenage boy. We were separated and the yelling eventually ceased. He was kicked off the team and the season went on.

I was charged by his parents with physical and verbal assault, which was later thrown out of court. This was the worst time of my coaching and teaching career. I lost emotional control but I put the blame on the kid. Many people who knew the situation thought that it was entirely his fault. He was the one who would not listen. He lost his cool with an adult and coach who was trying to make him follow orders. For the next couple of years, I didn't regret any part of my role in the incident. If he had listened, it wouldn't have gone that far.

I started my Self-directed Shift and came to realize the extent of my own role. I lost control and I created that situation or I could have changed the outcome through my own actions. I understand now that if I had lost my job, it wouldn't have been his fault. It would have been mine because I had the power to control my actions by not letting my emotions dictate my steps. I met him at a local bar on his twenty-first birthday and gave one of the most sincere apologies I have ever given to a person. I was not just apologizing to him. I had recognized who I was, who I am, and who I was becoming. I started understanding "the self" in self-awareness.

There's a hurricane out there again. They always threaten to break the routines of our lives. Living here on the Mississippi Coast, we have become accustomed to these interruptions in our life during hurricane season. The Gulf is not the only place where storms are brewing. Inside the hearts and minds of each one of us are storms. They are those emotions and internal conflicts that guide us and drive us. Some are raging Category Five disasters waiting to happen, and others are isolated thunderstorms that pop up unexpectedly and are soon replaced by the warm sunshine peering through the clouds.

Yesterday a mild tropical depression was spotted off the coast of my soul. I had to battle the wind and rain. I even had to board up my windows. My Friday morning was not off to a particularly great start but I was determined to have a good day. Even though I was a little down, I gave myself a great self-talk as I drove into work. By the time I got to school, got a bite to eat and started addressing my class for the morning, I had the blues just about kicked. That is, until she opened her mouth. We will call her "Negative Nelly". With her, the glass is always half empty. During the course of the period, every time I would address her or the class, she would reply with her usually oppositional and cynical answers. I do not dislike her or anything like that, because I have accepted her pessimistic and combative personality.

This day was a different day. There was a storm inside of my body ready to make landfall. There was a battle to protect myself from the negative feelings and the fleeing positive attitude. From all of my reading, I knew the situation was under my control; and my feelings and attitude were up to me. This particular day, for some reason, was a struggle. The struggle was not with that student. It was a personal struggle; one that had not shown up for some time. I could have given up and resorted to my old personal self by letting my attitude get the best of me. I could have stopped fighting from within and given in to the negativity that would have surely ruined my whole day. I finally won the battle and let go. Sometimes we have to fight the internal storm that tries to fester within us. We must gather all of our supplies and head for higher ground. Sometimes we have to board the windows and prepare the sandbags for the waters that threaten to flood us. We are warned by the emotions that threaten to derail us. Sometimes the warnings are shorter than others but we must take heed, prepare and fight to protect ourselves from ourselves. Your emotions can be blessings that work for you, or they can be a curse that will take you far away from where you want to be.

I choose to take the approach that I need you ... or one day I will. You never know. We are relational beings. We need each other. Part of our human make-up is being connected to each other and depending on goods, services, thoughts, prayers and the lending hands of others for our survival and wellbeing. We have to be careful of the relationships we destroy today. We have to be aware of the ramifications of our actions as we deal with one another. I try to treat my students and others as if one day my life may be in their hands. What if the person you cross in some evil way has to serve you in a restaurant years later? Will they remember the foul acts you bestowed upon them and return the favor? Do you even want to take that chance? What if that young teenager that you "can't stand" and have problems with is the EMT that first responds to an accident that involves you? I never know when I will be in a vulnerable position where you will have a direct impact on my life, so I choose to keep our relationship in good standing. I try to win friends and influence people in positive ways. I wish not to alienate myself from others. Even in differing opinions, we should be compassionate to others and not make enemies if we can avoid it. Try not to burn bridges because you never know, that co-worker that you constantly argue with may end up being your boss.

CHAPTER 5

Success and Dreams

"Success is the progressive realization of a worthy goal or ideal."

–Earl Nightingale

The Self-directed Shift is success itself. Just stepping onto the path that most people don't and moving forward embodies what success is. It is the progressive realization of a worthy idea or cause. It's more about the journey than the end result. You have to be moving forward in the right direction. That direction is the one you intentionally choose. It is creating a shift that is different from what is normal because you want results that are not normal or typical of the average Joe.

Can you look in the mirror and say, "I'm a successful person"? You can if you are going through life doing your very best. Success should not be measured by winning or losing. Everyone can't win the race, but everyone can be successful in the race if they gave all that they could. Each one of us will achieve differently. I have three sons and I am preparing for the fact that each one may venture into different fields of study or they may take different paths in life. It would be hard to determine the most successful of the three by the degrees they achieve, the careers they choose, the money they earn, the houses they live in, or the cars they drive. Their success will be measured by how well they live up to their potential.

As a high school teacher, I see this drawn out year to year. The most successful student in my classroom may be the D-Student who pushes and pushes to make a C. It may be a student with some type of learning disability who works harder than everyone else to make average grades. Tommy may be very smart and talented. He may have a natural gift to succeed without very much effort; but where is his success? Does he produce above and beyond the abilities God has given him, or is he just getting by because his aptitude is higher than everyone else's? Some will go off to major universities, get great high paying jobs, live seemingly good lives and have children who fall into that same pattern. I am not knocking them, but I see doctors, lawyers, scientists and engineers walking the halls every day and I am not very impressed at those careers they will achieve. I see their lifestyles; all that their parents provide. They are blessed with opportunity. At seventeen they drive better cars than most of the teachers. Good for them, but I am impressed by those struggling in life at seventeen years old, but still make it. I'm impressed by those with the silver spoons, who don't use wealth as a crutch for their success. Those that are promised a jail cell but end up being a corrections officer. I'm impressed by the young lady who got pregnant, and still goes to community college and gets her associates degree. Success to me is getting more out of life than the cards that were dealt to you.

We should honor and praise those people pushing themselves to do the best they can even though the best they can. may be average. When I was just a kid in high school, I overheard Coach Brown, my football coach, say that those are the ones we should really be paying attention to. Most of those high A students are going to leave for the big cities in search for greener pastures; but the average kids who work hard and give their personal best are the ones who will replenish our community. I see successful people every day working right here in my hometown; but I see unsuccessful people as well doing the same jobs. I say they are unsuccessful because they can be doing so much more. I see very talented people that have the potential to be doing much more. God put you here to do something special. Are you doing it? John Wooden states that

you'll feel good about yourself if you're trying your hardest because you know you gave it your all. Being successful is the feeling of personal achievement from knowing you gave it your best effort.

Are you dreaming? Have your dreams faded away with age? Maybe something or someone has stifled your dreams. You may need to start dreaming again. There is nothing wrong with dreaming big and wanting more out of life than what you are receiving. We must still be thankful for all that we currently have while dreaming of the greatness God has in store for you.

I've been dreaming my whole life. I remember my mind wandering and the wishful thinking day to day. I always wanted something that others had; those with situations that were much better than mine. I dreamed of the life I wanted to live and all that fits inside of that life. All of those things have not yet been accomplished but my feet are planted firmly on the yellow brick road that will take me there. It is no coincidence that I live in a house that is three times as big as the project apartments I once called home. I dreamed of a big house with a yard and room to raise a family. There is no coincidence that my wife is the most beautiful, loving and caring woman in the world. I dreamed of her when I was just a young man and asked God to send her to me one day. It may be hard to imagine a young boy dreaming of a great marriage with a great lady and wonderful children. I did. I dreamed, like many young boys, of being a professional athlete, playing on television and being a star. Early in high school, I dreamed of one day teaching and coaching in that very same school. In the third grade, I dreamed of writing books and sharing them with the world. Many of my dreams have come true and many are still being formed. To this day I still dream. I am not afraid of letting my mind imagine all of the possibilities that my heart desires. I believe in the magic of dreaming big. It is the only thing that I believe separates what I have done in my life from those who have accomplished less. It is the power of a dream, believing in it, and putting forth the effort to make it reality. If you are not motivated to get up and move, get a bigger dream. Take the time to ask yourself, "What if?" Money isn't holding you back. It's not talent, intelligence, looks or even luck. It's your reluctance to dream and believe. Everything I've accomplished, everything I have, and everything that will come to me has started as a dream. Everything that you will receive in this life will manifest first from a dream.

One night I read books with my sons and one particular story stood out as I read with my youngest, Larkin. It was "Mickey's Christmas Carol". You should know the story well by now except there were Disney characters playing all of the parts. It played an eerie parallel to my life. Scrooge was a wealthy but bitter ol' man. He didn't treat those around him particularly nice. You see, I was a wealthy man. Not with money, but with the riches of an abundant life that God has seen fit to bless me with. I have a job that most admire. I have a wife so beautiful and sweet that none other can compare to. God has blessed me with three healthy male heirs to my throne. The spirits have constantly brought me back and forth to the past and to my future through my conscious mind. I was once a happy youngster with the biggest dreams and hopes for my future. I was to be the savior of my family; the one who would do great things and be adored by many and loved by all. Fame was sure to come. Material success was inevitable. The sky was truly the limit.

Something happened inside of me that have happened to millions of people in this world. I stopped dreaming and stopped believing in a life so much more than mere existence. Something took my spirit and showed me a future of mine that would be similar to thousands upon thousands of Americans today. It was a future of strained marital relations, financial turmoil, unhealthy eating habits, a career heading nowhere and becoming my crutch, spiraling alcohol consumption, absentee fatherhood similar to that of my own, and a gambling addiction that would eventually cripple an already dying purse. Like the character Scrooge, I went into a panic. " I can Change! Let me Change!" My present state of mind is different because of the thought of what could be my future. I have regained that vision, passion and purpose that I had as a young man fighting hard to have better outcomes in life. I will not become a part of the divorce rate. I will raise my boys to be men. Heart disease and diabetes will not rear their ugly faces my way. I will not live paycheck to paycheck. I will have a great attitude towards myself and to others. There will be no more pity parties in my head because of what I have not yet achieved. I will achieve every dream and reach every goal that enters into my mind. I will not fall to the pitfalls of drugs, alcohol or gambling. You may also adopt this philosophy and secure your future. Develop yourself in every area of life. Start by choosing one area that needs improvement and attack it. Turn the television off! Scratch the radio station! Start reading books and listening to self-help materials. Personal development and self-help is the key to your future. Let me help you live the life you've always wanted!

There are some people who are truly happy with their life. It is definitely a blessing to be living in this world healthy, fed, and with a roof over your head. I am grateful for all that God has provided for me. We live in the richest part of this world at the richest time in history. If you are reading this, your life is probably 100 times greater than over half of the people that are on this planet. Name your problem. Speak of the cross that you must carry and I'll bet you $100 to a bucket of spit that there are millions of others who would trade their life for yours.

With all of that said, it doesn't mean that you have to settle for less than what you deserve. There is nothing wrong with dreaming big and wanting the better things out of life. Too often I see people rationalizing about why they have so little. We have been made to believe that living paycheck to paycheck, cupboards being empty at the end of the month, being in debt, financing everything and building someone else's dreams is normal as long as you have your health.

Tell your kids not to dream big. Tell them now, while they are young, not to aim high. Teach them to settle for a mediocre job that they really don't want but will pay their bills. Let's teach our babies to work for minimum wages, to stay at home and not see what the entire world has to offer. We don't do that. We tell our kids that they can be anything that they want to be. We tell them that they can be millionaires, astronauts, and even president. The sky is the limit. We dream build with our kids on large scales, and then at some point we start telling them to settle and be happy for what they have. So many adults shut their dreams down and aim to help their kids reach theirs. As those kids get older, they start settling and decide to help their kids make it. The cycle never ends. Someone has to step up and make big accomplishments.

My children must see me accomplish big goals in my life. Even if I don't reach them, they must see me fighting for them and not giving up on things that are attainable but tough. I thank God everyday for this life I live. God wants you to prosper. He wants you to have an abundance of wealth so that you can better serve his kingdom. I know that you are serving God now but imagine serving him and his people with three or four times the resources that you have now. Stop telling yourself that you are doing fine when you are not. Be thankful for all that you have, but know that it is okay to want more out of life. Know that it is okay to strive for those things that you may think are out of your reach. People have those things and some are less deserving than you.

Teaching video production to high school students has been an amazing experience. As they choose topics and story lines for their movie projects, they get stuck. Even in groups they can't find the direction they want to go. I tell them to think about their favorite movies. Think about those epic movies that we all love. There is a pattern that is repeated time and time again. Dream-Struggle-Victory. Every day I watch people keep their heads just above the struggle. We lose sight of our dream; we are afraid to struggle; and even more, we can't let someone else see us struggle. We never see the victory of our dream. We can't take steps backwards that will ultimately propel us forward even faster. Victory only comes after a struggle, a fight, or a war. The bigger the dream, the bigger the struggle you will have.

As a nation, we have stopped fighting. Instant gratification has ruined our chances at Victory. It has stopped us from dreaming. What can I have now? If this attitude continues, you will always float just above water. I ask people "How are you doing?" every day and the overwhelming response is " I'm making it. I can't complain." The statistics say that most of us are just making it. I want to hear that you are doing excellent. I want you to at least be on the verge of a great victory! Where are your dreams? Are they lost? Have you thrown them away with yesterday's garbage? Find them, build new ones, and dedicate yourself to them. Yes, you will struggle if your dream is big enough, but it will be worth it. Tell someone you trust. Tell a friend who believes in you. Seek counsel and find out what it will take to make your dreams come true. Fight through the struggles of life to get your victory. I see a lot of you going back to school and struggling with work, kids, and balancing the whole act. I am proud of you. Keep fighting. Your struggle will lead to victory. What is comfortable now becomes uncomfortable later. What is uncomfortable now becomes comfortable later. The struggle is just a phase but you must purposely struggle by denying yourself now so that your dream can be secured. Delay your gratification and develop your long-term vision. Build your dream, accept the struggle that is to come with its realization, and get your victory!

Today go out and dream build. I will revisit those dreams that once raged inside of you. Visit the neighborhood that you would like to purchase a home in. Test drive your dream car. Research what it will take to get into the school of your choice. It's okay to start looking at wedding dresses and dreaming of the day that you will walk down the aisle even if you don't have the ideal mate ready to meet you at the altar just yet. Develop new dreams because life has changed and there are victories you want, need and deserve in your life. The dream can be real. Dreams can become a reality, but a reality can't become, until it is first a dream in the heart and the mind of a dreamer. The greatest dreamers are those who are not asleep. Wake up!

"The idea of dream building insinuates action. Thus, it requires one to take the dream that the Great Architect-God- places within and to become builder on the planet. For me "dream building requires that my dreams be written on paper through vision boards and placed where they are easily seen. I need to see them every day as a reminder of where I am going, what I am capable of, and what I need to do to accomplish the dreams. That plus my faithfulness to walk in my purpose and dutifulness to my work has provided uplift and afforded me the opportunity I have to serve in my dream position. In James 2:17, it states,

"Even so faith, if it hath not works, is dead, being alone." In other words, put feet on your dreams, and get to work!"

Dr. Carla J. Evers, Superintendent

Pass Christian Schools

CHAPTER 6

Seeing Further Down the Road

"Change is the law of life. And those who look only to the past or present are certain to miss the future."

John F. Kennedy

By now the idea should be in your head. Building success and creating a Self-directed Shift in your life has nothing to do with talent, luck, I.Q. or any inherent gift. It doesn't take a physical ability or knowhow. It should be apparent the shift starts in the mind with our thinking, beliefs and dreams of the future self we want to become. There are many key principles to success. One of the most vital is long-term vision.

I have to live with the decisions that I have made and the actions that I have done in the past. We all need to understand that our lives today are made from what we did yesterday. Some of the things that I have done and the decisions I made when I was younger will fade and the consequences of those actions will no longer be relevant in my life today. Some of those actions and decisions, good or poor, will yield residual effects forever. There are things that will always remain and constantly produce fruit, good or bad. A fact of life is that we can't change the past or what we did. We can only change the future. We have the power of predicting the future by our actions today. What we do in this moment is what we will gain tomorrow, good or bad. The path we put our foot on today will lead us to that place where we will rest our feet tomorrow. That place may be pleasant or not so! That choice is ours. We just have to see so much further down the road. Predicting your future and gaining the things, relationships and outcomes you desire is about having long-term vision. That long-term vision is what should control your actions today. Today's actions are not about today. They are about tomorrow. My focus is further down the road right now because I am living a life today from the decisions I made years ago. Some were good and some were not so! I know that the only way for me to get to a great present in the future is to make the right decisions today for tomorrow.

I am burdened in life by the wrong choices I have made. They haunt me every day. "If I would have", "I could have", and "I should have" are all phrases that I heard from the older people in my life when I was a child. They are the words that rattle in my brain today as I think of the opportunities I had in the past but squandered because I didn't understand delayed gratification. It's putting off what you can have today so that you can have much more of an abundance tomorrow. It is about the future. I still struggle with it some today as many people do. I haven't left those mistakes behind because they are what motivate me.

Of all the principles of success I have studied, Long-Term Vision stands so bright and vivid. If you could somehow see past what's right in front of your face and see miles down the road, you can do the things that will not have you questioning your actions years from now. "Would've", "could've", and "should've" won't be spoken on your lips. If God grants me the time to see old age, I refuse to live it in struggle. I see too many people who are at the point where they should be enjoying life, relaxing, vacationing, playing with grandkids, traveling the globe, but instead they are working their fingers to the bone, trying to survive and waiting on a social security check. That's not the life I plan to live. That's not the life I want to see you live. We have to make better choices. I'm talking to myself even more than I am talking to you.

It's a struggle to deny all that you want and all that you think you need so that you can have even more for yourself and to give to others later. From the vehicle I drive to the clothes I wear and the cell phone I carry, they all have a purpose towards the future I am creating. I can't afford to make the same mistakes over and over and expect different results. Time is not standing still. I only ask that God continue to grant me this good life with a wonderful wife, awesome children, a passion for what I do and continue to help me stay on path for a great future. Keep me on my Self-directed Shift. I was not put here to live an average life. Neither were you. You were created to live life to its fullest by creating the life you choose by the choices you make.

I had to speak one Sunday morning in the church I grew up in as a young boy. I was somewhat nervous from the stares of familiar faces. Earlier that morning I struggled with what clothes to wear. I paced undecidedly and toiled between wearing a suit jacket or not. Something kept telling me to wear the jacket. I thought it might have made me seem a little more respectable wearing the coat as I spoke, so I did. Driving to that church, I couldn't decide what to talk about as a lead-in to the purpose of me being there. A voice kept saying, "the coat, the coat...."! I didn't understand at first but then it hit me. Twenty years ago I met the most influential man on my life. He became my friend, my spiritual mentor, and my father. He raised me right there in that church from a boy to a man. It took a while but he did. I give much honor to Fr. Armand Francis Theriault, SVD. Without him coming into my life, almost none of the fruits that I have produced would have come about.

One day a priest friend of his died and Father Theriault received his clothes. Among those clothes was a grey suit that he gave to me. I had never owned a suit. As a sixteen years old boy, my wardrobe consisted of t-shirts and ratty old jeans. I didn't have a suit of my own so I was proud to accept it, but the suit didn't fit. He told me that one-day it would. I would grow into it. The sleeves hung to the middle of my hands, the jacket was at the middle of my thighs and the pants were pretty baggy but I wore it anyway. I wore that suit to every function I could think of. I just changed the shirt and tie. It didn't matter how big it was; I had a suit. I look through all of my pictures over the years and I have on that suit. As I grew older, I started filling out and the suit started fitting a little better. I even wore that suit to my mother's wedding some years later.

My mentor knew that one day that suit would fit. He saw further down the road. Sometimes people give us things. It may be a suit, it may be helpful information, or it may be tools to help us succeed. It may not fit right now. You may not understand why they are giving it to you or you may not want it because it doesn't quite fit in your life right now. We have to look past today and past the things that are uncomfortable and look further down the road. How will this help me later? Our vision should not be limited to what we can physically see, but what can and will be years from now. That vision gives us the direction for today. I stood there at the altar telling the story of the suit that was given to me twenty years earlier. I tugged on the lapels of my coat and proclaimed, " This is the suit. Today it fits!" How far are you looking ahead? What can you see in your mind for the future that may not be visible with your eyes?

Stephen Covey says it best. Begin with the end in mind. Where do you want to be? Where do you want to go? If you don't know where you're going, any road will take you there. Your past is not your future, but your present-day actions, attitudes and thought process will dictate your future results. I had a conversation with one of my colleagues during one of our regular twenty-minute lunch breaks. A few of us teachers lock the doors at lunch, take a deep breath and take off the teacher's hat that we so elegantly wear. To that other teacher's surprise, I was not always the person who stands before you today. I teach at the same high school that I almost didn't graduate from as a student. The principal, who at one point did not see me fit to walk for graduation, was the instrumental factor in me getting hired at my Alma Mater some ten years later. I am not ashamed of who I was or the things that I have done in my past. They are the elements that have shaped and molded me into the person I am today.

Growth and change is a significant part of what I propagate today. I can't deny who I was and the path that my actions were leading me on. Most people would be shocked at some of my life stories, because they only know Mr. Lewis, the teacher and coach. It may be hard to wrap your mind around the sixteen year old who threw the first punch in every brawl, the young man wandering the streets at two or three o'clock in the morning looking for trouble, or the lost soul breaking into your house while you slept quietly in your bed. Amazingly, I don't even wish to forget those things. They are reminders of how far I have come. How far are you willing to go? What are you willing to let go? The gold teeth and the bad attitude are gone. They demonstrate my growth and the change that has taken place in my life.

The physical transformation has long been over. Now the change is more spiritual, mental, emotional and psychological. The change is happening from within; deeper than any part of my being that has ever been touched. There was no near-death experience; I didn't have a "Come to Jesus" moment; and I didn't face losing everything I had. I just wanted better results out of my life for my family, friends, and myself. It does not matter what road you traveled. It does not matter the path that you were once on. You just need to decide to get on a different path. You need to get on a path that can lead to the future you want. You need to create a Self-directed Shift. Anyone can change. A life of true happiness and abundance is available for everyone who wants it. You need only to decide on your course. Today look back on your life and see where it has brought you. Look at the place where you currently stand, visualize where your direction is taking you, and decide exactly where you would like to be. Do the thing that is necessary to change your direction. Become the person you always wanted to be and live the life you were meant to live.

We must look to the future and focus on where we want to go, but someday is not a future word. Neither is one day or even tomorrow. Those days don't exist. Today is the day you need to put emphasis on. Today is the day. Millions of people are hanging their hats on Someday. Time keeps on ticking and Someday is just as far away from you now as it was several years ago. We are all guilty at some point in our lives of waiting on that day to arrive. Someday never will! You are already blessed far more than you can imagine. You have everything you need right now. You do have the time, money and other vital resources to achieve every accomplishment you desire.

There's not going to be some big event that will magically catapult you into success. You can't sit back and wait for your lucky numbers to be called. How many people say that someday they will win that lottery and how many actually do? They know that's not going to happen, but it gives then some sense of comfort in that moment. It's a short-lived moment.

You already have the winning ticket. You just can't see it. You're not looking in the right places. If it's not huge, we don't want it. If something big doesn't happen, we don't believe in the possibility of it getting accomplished. Successful people know that it does not take something big to make a difference. It takes little things done consistently over long periods of time. It takes little steps not giant leaps. How do you eat an Elephant? You do it one bite at a time. Whatever it is you would like to accomplish or be successful at, start today. Don't wait on Someday. It's not on the calendar. It's not this month or any other month this year. I call it "Neveruary". Someday I will lose twenty pounds. No you won't unless today you take a step towards that goal. Someday I will become a nurse or get my bachelor's degree. I don't think so unless you sign up for classes today. Someday when I get the down payment, I will buy that new house. You will be renting for the rest of your life unless you start today by putting away something for your new house. Do little things over a period of time that can lead you to your destination.

I've come to realize that Ten years is not a long time. The time flies. My wife and I were married twelve years ago and dated a few years before that. Where has the time gone? It has ticked away one second, minute and week at a time. Twelve years just didn't instantly happen. Let's look at the next ten years of your life. Put away just $15 a week and you will have almost $8000 in ten years. Imagine doing that and every couple of months you added an extra twenty. That's over $10,000 accumulated small amounts at a time. Think about the money you waste every week on all the things you don't need. Start a ten-year plan with the little dollars you spend on honey buns, cokes, candy bars and chips. You would be amazed.

"Someday" you are not going to be rich. "Someday" you are not going to get in shape. "Someday" you are not going to do anything. You have to do it today. Do something small towards your goals, but do it consistently over a long period of time. The day will come when you look at your ticket and can honestly say, " I won!". Shift your thinking to an attitude of "Today". Your Self-directed Shift starts today.

The realization that all of the decisions and actions occurring in one's life have affected us to some degree is a major step in the Self-directed Shift that Rickey Lewis refers to in this chapter. Rickey's ability to see, understand and potentially act on the opportunity for personal and professional growth has been present throughout our 20 plus year relationship. Our pre-draft conversations before him signing his first professional baseball contract with the Milwaukee Brewers organization in 1998, along with numerous conversations we have had over the years reflected his ability to see things from a long-term perspective, but he had not completely worked out the kinks regarding understanding that the decisions you make moving forward have power to take you where you want to go can be enlightening and empowering. Negative experiences are rarely easy to set aside and ignore, and they occasionally fail to offer any life lessons, but I am encouraging you to open your minds to the possibility that the optimism and hope being shared in this chapter might help you avoid pitfalls and embrace charting a new path for yourself.

Jonathan Story,

Former MLB Baseball Scout and

Current Assistant Principal

CHAPTER 7

Strengthen Your Faith, Secure Your Life

"In order to have faith in his own path, he does not need to prove that someone else's path is wrong."

- Paulo Coelho, Warrior of the Light

Faith is defined as confidence or trust in a person or thing. It's a belief in something that is not based on proof. Faith can be described as the teachings of a particular religion or belief in God. Whether you have faith or not, believe in God, The Universe, or any other power higher than man, there are principles that govern this world. Principles are forever. They are absolute and unchanging through time. These principles can be found in what I believe to be the greatest book ever written or the greatest collection of writings ever put together that are principle-centered. That book is the Bible.

Whether you believe in God, Christ or the historical context of the Bible, there are absolute principles on every page from cover to cover. Beneath the stories of the bible and between the lines of text are the greatest clues and keys to your success. There are many books with principle-centered messages, but the bible carries them all. There is no principle that will lead you to success in any area of your life that is not found inside of it. The Bible or the scriptures from it will have to become part of your study and influence. Often we will be indirectly influenced by God's word through people who are immersed in it.

Friday, December 21, 2012 at 9:18 A.M. would be the last time that I would hear his voice. Sitting in a hotel room in the cold mountains of Tennessee, I reflect back on that last conversation. It was not a special one at the time. It was very much like every other phone call we shared every two weeks or so. It was not very long, it was heartfelt, honest and ended in "I love you Father".

When your phone rings early in the morning and the number is a loved one who doesn't often call, you know that this call is special. In the moments it took for the phone to ring three or four times, a small fear of the unknown crossed my mind. When I was told of the passing of Father T, the fear immediately left. I know that if anyone sits in heaven, if anyone deserves the glory of the Kingdom of God, and if anyone has truly earned the right to walk among the angels, it's Father Armand Francis Xavier Theriault, SVD.

He was not my first mentor and he is not my last; but he has been my most influential. God couldn't have picked a more perfect time to put him in my life. I was sixteen years old and our first meeting was of him bringing me a Christmas gift because my name was placed on an angel tree at church. I accepted his gift, but I asked him for a job. And so the teaching began.

Being a mentor is a great responsibility, and being mentored is just as big. The two have to be willing to give of themselves to ensure the success and growth of each person and their relationship. I don't know how it happened but it did. Early on it was a struggle because neither one of us would budge. I'm so grateful that he never did. Something in my thick skull realized that I needed what he was willing to teach. He held no punches (figuratively and literally). Not to discount the number of people who touched my life, but he did more for me in becoming the man I am today than any other person my life has seen. He taught me how to become wealthy even though he took a vow of poverty. He taught me how to love my wife even though he has never been married. He taught me how to be a father to my children even though he had no biological children of his own. We developed a strong bond as Priest and lost soul, father and son, teacher and student, and friends. We wrote many papers in high school, we bought many cars, and we even had to cry over a girlfriend or two. Mainly I cried and he said, "I told you so". He was the first person to recognize that Lauren, my wife, would be my rock. He knew she was perfect for me before I knew, because he knew me better than I knew myself. He married us and baptized our firstborn.

Six months before God called him home, I got to see him one last time, and he got to see my two youngest sons for the first time. Their lives will be better because of the life he instilled in me. There's not enough paper and pencils to write all of the things he has done for me, the wisdom he shared, or the times he made me stand up and be a man. I was not the first young man he put under his wings, and I was not the last.

His whole life was dedicated to serving God and making a real impact on the lives of young and old, just like he did with a young sixteen year old who didn't just get a gift for Christmas, but got a gift for life. God was working through him. Father had been filled with the spirit and taught all of those principles of the Bible to a kid who was not close to God. I had not been very religious, but tried walking the straight path of righteousness because of him. God took care of me through Father Theriault and I didn't quite realize how that was working until I got older. This message is not really to honor "Father T", because I choose to honor him by living the life he was preparing me for. This message is for you. Find your "Father T". If you are lost, looking for direction, need a mentor or just a really good friend who can bring you closer to God, His word and the true principles found in the Bible, find your "Father T". Find those individuals who have fruit on the tree in the area of faith. They can draw you closer to God.

A few years ago I read "RESOLVED: 13 Resolutions for LIFE" by Orrin Woodward. It encouraged me to build my own resolutions to develop a better groundwork and game plan for my own growth and the growth of my family. The resolutions were not to be like most New Year's resolutions we think about. It wasn't to lose weight, stop eating junk food, or go to the gym three days a week. Those are often resolutions for actions that quickly fade by February. I'm talking about resolutions built on principles that build tremendous growth and personal development in your life by studying them and applying them every day. I built my resolutions around the cornerstones of who we are.

The first Resolution of mine that I knew must be addressed was my faith. Our overall growth will be dictated in how strong we can build our faith and belief system of a power greater than ourselves.

RESOLUTION 1: "Every night and morning, pray to God. Get on my knees every time I pray. Have everyone in the house pray on his or her knees. Talk to God and give him praise for all that he has done. Stop talking to God only when things are hard or when we need a miracle. Go to church every week even if I don't feel up to it, if I am tired, sleepy, or in doubt. Teach my sons by example. Read the Bible. Seek meaning and help in God's word. Talk with people with strong faith to gain a deeper faith. In every decision, think about Jesus and God's opinion of my actions."

A lot of people went to church and prayed for those children and teachers who lost their lives in the Newtown Elementary School shooting. A lot of people hugged their own children and asked God to protect them from that kind of evil. A resolution that we all should implement is to pray every day and stop asking for God's grace only in times of need and sorrow. Build your life on resolutions rich in principles and strong in faith. Talk to God, praise God, and ask for His mercy every day. Looking to God only when times are hard makes me believe you don't think you need him every day. We truly need the grace of God.

One Sunday I found myself sitting in a church pew with a piece of paper and a pen for the first time. A few weeks ago I was struck by something the priest read from the Gospel and talked about in his sermon. Being struck by the word is not something new to me or to many people who attend church services. It doesn't matter what faith you follow or your religious preference. It is very easy to be motivated or inspired on issues of faith when it is the person's job who is preaching, to do just that. After church I asked the pastor for his notes and he immediately stated that he would email them to me. By Tuesday I had not received them and I could not, for the life of me, remember what had me fired-up on Sunday. That is typical for me and I dare to say, for a lot of people living in this world. Church, God and all of that religious stuff, was for Sunday mornings. My faith and actions did not find themselves living in my heart Monday through Saturday. Consequently, the results of my actions were not of the caliber that I would have liked to have.

Back to the paper and pen. I am introducing a self-directed education into every area of my life including faith. I venture to say that I was the only person in my church taking notes. You may not have to take notes. I have to take notes to remember and study. If there is a question, I can look up that information for myself. I can educate myself in faith and create a self-directed shift. I have learned a lot in my faith by simply going to church on Sundays and some things naturally sticking. What if we purposely study and grow in faith; search for meaning behind the teachings of the faith we follow? Many people go to church as a routine or habit. I've gone to church more in the past year than I have ever gone in any year's span in my life. Yes, it's part of my routine, but that is where I needed to start. I wanted a stronger faith, so I've had to force myself to get up and go every Sunday, no matter what. Once you have committed to the process, the shift can happen. Study your faith. Don't just take what your pastor, priest, rabbi or minister tells you as truth. Be autonomous in your thinking. Your studies and self-directed education may draw you deeper into your faith or it may steer you in a different direction, but it will be a path that you intentionally follow. Be purposeful in all of your actions, ideas, and convictions.

We see celebrities walking the red carpet wearing beautiful dresses, tailor-made suits, and stunning tuxedoes created by world famous designers. No longer are they questioned on what they are wearing but who they are wearing. The emphasis is on the creator more so than the outfit. Pay close attention to the next red-carpet event you see on television and listen for that question, "Who are you wearing?" I'm sure you will hear names such as Oscar de la Renta, Vera Wang, Versace, Dolce & Gabbana and Michael Kors to name a few.

Now ask yourself, who are you wearing? Are you wearing God's three-piece suit or formal gown that he has designed for you? Can others tell that you are dressed in the fabric of God? Maybe you are not dressed up right now. Your attire is hanging in the closet waiting for the right moment. The right moment is now. It's every day of your life. You should be dressed in the Lord. Put on God in a new way. Show the world who your designer is. Maybe it doesn't fit. You can grow into that suit. He made it big because he wants you to grow. Just start wearing it. Put it on. Don't worry, he's going to help you fit into that dress. He wants you to work out and lose some of those habits so that it will fit perfectly. Take off those jeans, t-shirts and old shoes. You're on the red carpet and everyone's watching. Lights. Camera. Action. Who are you wearing? You don't have to say. Others can tell.

There truly is a higher power willing and ready to help you in your Self-directed Shift. You need only to have faith that He who has given you life will help you attain all that you need as well as what you want. I did say help. You have to initiate the process and be intentional in your pursuit of increasing your faith that draws you closer to the principles you need to be a success.

The Bible tells us that faith comes by hearing and by the Word of God. You can't say you have strong faith, if you don't spend time reading and hearing God's written or spoken word!! Get the bible app on your phone and start a reading plan. If you don't like to read, there's an option on the app that allows the app to read to you. Take notes in church and read the notes aloud throughout the week. Make hearing God's Word A priority because we must build our faith

Lp (Like Paul)

Motivational Speaker, Licensed Minister (Youth Specialist)

CHAPTER 8

Financial Intelligence

"The only way you will ever permanently take control of your financial life is to dig deep and fix the root problem."

-*Suze Orman*

Reading books and listening to audios has become one of my new passions. Not just any materials, but materials with the power to change the way you think and see life. As I learn, the more I want to learn. The more I read, the more I uncover hidden truths that have evaded me thus far in my life. Receiving this new information is bringing me to the realization that I could never get to the place where I wanted to be. School, the streets, or mama didn't teach me. None of those have the results that I am looking for. So I read. Not the new vampire series. Not the Hunger Games Trilogy. I read from books that have shaped the lives of many, seeking the same knowledge and committed to thinking differently.

Finances are a big issue in the lives of most people I come into contact with and almost no one seems to have a good handle on it. Those who may be doing well are not screaming their secrets from the mountaintops. My problem is that I haven't been taught financial principles by anyone close to me who has watched me struggle over the years. That's because just about everyone in my circle was struggling too.

We have to change the way we think. We have to learn from those who have made their way from the bottom to the top. The answer is not making more money. The money that you are making right now is probably good enough to start building wealth beyond your current status and to secure yourself for life. At some point you need to read Robert Kiyosaki's *"Rich Dad Poor Dad"* and *"Cashflow Quadrant"*. THE ABSOLUTE MUST READ for every man, woman and child is *"The Richest Man in Babylon"*. Read Napoleon Hill's *"Think and Grow Rich"*. *"God's Plans for Your Finances"* by Dwight Nichols is a great start on building wealth with biblical principles that we are not taught in Sunday School!

If you are broke and can't seem to get things going, go get these books. If you really want to change your lean purse into a fat purse, go get these books. If you think God doesn't want you to be wealthy, go get these books. If you have a financial goal and you don't know how to reach it, go get these books. The amount of information I've received from books on increasing my financial intelligence and leading to my financial freedom far exceeds anything anyone has told me.

It was hard to believe that I would hand a financial book to a broke person looking for financial help and they wouldn't read it. It amazed me the number of people who wouldn't listen to one of my financial audios who clearly needed the information. If you are looking to create a Self-directed Shift in your finances, you are going to have to read, listen and associate with people well versed in finances. If you are not willing to do these things, you really don't want the change you say you want.

A female student of mine told me that I should talk to her eighteen-year-old boyfriend. She wants me to help him get rich. That's pretty ambitious! Don't help me. Help the man who will take care of me. I laughed and didn't say what I was thinking. I just pointed to a book that was on my desk just a few feet away. I grabbed it and said this is all he needs. If only I could have read it at eighteen!

That book has got to be the best book ever written on how to gain wealth from where you are and financial principles that are easy to understand and apply in your life. It truly is the most inspiring book on wealth ever written. George S. Clason wrote the book in 1926. That book is " *The Richest Man in Babylon*".

Ever since I've began my journey of learning and studying as much as I can about every aspect of life that we are governed by, I decided that my sons would receive this information well before the age that I received it. The first two books I planned to read to them were "*The Magic of Thinking Big*" by David J. Schwartz and this one. This one has been on my mind since I suggested it to that student. I knew that I was going to attempt to read it to my oldest son Landon before bed that night. He had just turned eight a few days earlier. He's starting to "dig" money, so what better time than now to start the money talks and teaching financial principles. He was all for me reading it to him but initially was disappointed because there were no pictures. I was amazed at how easily he was getting the concepts. It took me explaining some things in layman's terms but he got it. If an eight-year-old can get it, what about you? Maybe you don't need it. You've got this finance thing under control? I didn't have a clue.

Everything I was taught about money was wrong and that everything was not a lot. You can read this book in one day. It can change your perception on gaining wealth and you may just start applying the principles and become the Richest Man or Woman in your town. I read this book some time ago and without earning more income, the wealth of my family has grown and continues to grow. It came from knowledge that had evaded me my whole life. A seven- dollar book changed my thinking about money and has made me the master of my money instead of being a slave to it. I didn't and haven't stopped there. It sparked a thirst for more knowledge in the area of finances. It was a springboard towards my financial savvy, but this book can stand by itself. It's all you really need to take control. Take the chance and read this book.

My mission is not to solve your problems, but to point you in the right directions so that you may figure out ways to improve your life. Sometimes we just need a sign that points us the right way when we come to forks in the road. Your road to financial freedom can start today.

Friday. Pay day for a lot of people. "Another day and another dollar." Unfortunately, that dollar is spent before the check is even cashed. I had a really good talk with a friend of mine the other night. He used to have a thriving tire business some years ago. The business as it used to be, no longer exists. Selling tires and fixing leaky valve stems is just a side hustle now. He works as a custodian at a small elementary school, and conducts tire business after hours trying to make ends meet. As he put a set of very good used tires on my old truck, I couldn't help but to ask why was it that he was not really doing his tire business. He was and still is very passionate about tires. In his own words he claimed that the tire business is a gold mine.

In the conversation I found that it wasn't about the business failing or not making enough money. It was the same problem that most of the people I run across every day have. It was a lack of financial wisdom. We all believe we need to make more money. Making more would be nice, but that isn't going to solve the problems you're having. If you have a job with a steady flow of coins coming into your purse, it is a great start to you building your wealth and being able to live the lifestyle you would like to live.

Raise your hand if you're broke right now. It's okay. You're not alone. Most of us are broke and it's not because we don't make enough money. It's because we are spending more than we make. Simple, right! I made about $20,000 three years in a row. My salary jumped the fourth year to over $40,000. I was no better off financially though. I would even say that I was worse off. I had more things and more bills, but not a penny more towards a surplus of cash. I ended up in a hole. We learned to live off of that $20k, so why didn't the lifestyle continue into the new money? We are not programmed to live that way. We are programmed to spend just about all we make and now with credit, spend more than we make. When we get a raise, a job bonus, or an income tax check, we spend almost every nickel. How is it that so many people are broke, living paycheck to paycheck? It's just about everybody. Just about everybody I know! Don't say it's the economy because everyone makes different amounts but everyone is broke. We make different amounts but spend the same. We spend every dime.

Try getting all of your expenses to less than 75% of your net earnings. It may take six months or so but you can. Even if it takes a year or more, it will be worth it. You can live off of 75% because someone out there is making 75% of what you make and someone is making 75% of that person's salary. Every four months you will gain one month's salary. You can save 1 year's pay in just 4 years. It takes sacrifice but it can be done.

There are some great financial tools out there to help you. There are books and audios that can walk you through becoming wealthy. You can do it in a short period of time. The finances of my family have gotten better over the last year than it ever has been and we haven't gotten any raises. The only thing needed is an investment in the one tool God gave you. That tool is your brain. Gain the financial knowledge that is out there and use the wisdom. The wisdom is the application of what you learn. I have walked some people through and shown them the way to financial freedom and they won't move forward. I know it's hard and it may seem like nothing will work, but your freedom is right around the corner. You just have to want it bad enough.

I was tired of the cupboard being bare at the end of the month and waiting on payday. That's how it was growing up as a kid when there was only one income from my mother. My household income is about 5 times that and we were still living paycheck to paycheck. Something had to change. I see people every day driving nice cars, living in nice houses, wearing designer clothes, eating out all the time, and partying like a rock star, but have to borrow fifty dollars at the end of the month until next payday. That was me as well. Delay your gratification, live within your means, and find a way to raise your means.

You don't have to win a lottery, earn a six-figure salary, or get a big inheritance from a deceased uncle to achieve a millionaire's wealth. Read "The Millionaire Next Door". Most of us out there have the power to accumulate that kind of money only if we can understand how money works. We really don't understand. There are simple principles that can push you far past anything you could ever imagine.

The #1 principle that I have learned -- which was hard to grasp -- was to pay yourself first. You have to put you and your family at the top of the list of people to pay before all bills and obligations. If you don't, you will never get anywhere financially. That's from "The Richest Man in Babylon". You have to change your priorities. You don't have to make more money if you have a steady flow of income. You have to keep some of the money you already have. Spend less. Change your thinking. Believe that you deserve financial independence and that you will attain it. You can't have it all. Not right now at least. Your lifestyle has to be suitable to what you earn, not what Mr. Jones earns. Clearly define wants and needs. Even in a down economy there are so many ways to earn extra money. You could cell stuff on EBay, babysit, or do odd jobs for friends and neighbors. Humble yourself and get those dollars that are floating around out there.

Of all of my side jobs, anyone can do them. I have perfected my craft in making hustle money but I started out just as everyone else I knew. I didn't have a clue, but I was determined to make some cash. Making wise investments with the small amounts of money you have over time can explode your cash flow. Read "The Slight Edge" by Jeff Olson. Stay on the good side of the eighth wonder of the world, compound interest. Credit is a trap if it's not used properly and with lack of discipline. Eliminate Debt. Eliminate consumer debt. Asset debt is okay. Learn the difference. Consumer debt is like cancer eating away at your hard-earned money. Make a plan to succeed. Write your goals down and work towards them. I get tied of hearing people say, "just trying to make it". If you fail to plan, you plan to fail.

If you don't have a clue, get one! Start talking to people with financial success. Start reading financially empowering books. Study money and how it works as if your life depends on it because it does. People say money can't buy happiness. I know money isn't everything, but our world is based on money. It is the one thing that makes it go around. Even non-profit and missionary works have to be supported by money. Most people who complain about money don't truly understand how it works, how to accumulate it, how to multiply it or compound it. I'm blessed with an opportunity to teach teenagers true financial principles and increase their financial education. Are you broke? That's okay, if you are increasing your knowledge in money matters because money matters! If you are broke and you are doing nothing by the way of educating yourself out of poverty, there lies the problem.

How you are doing financially has a lot to do with how you think financially. How do you interpret information through your money views? Money is truly a mystery to most people. Most just don't understand it. Those who don't understand it think that people with a lot are lucky or they think that they cheated or scammed their way to riches. Money is a reward for proper thinking and proper action over a period of time.

If you are broke, struggling with finances and can't make ends meet, it's because you have chosen to be exactly what you are. You chose the exact financial situation that you are in. It was your choices that were either conscious or sub-conscious. You chose your financial life whether you knew you were choosing or not. The path that you are on is one that has been paved by you. The great thing about your situation is that you chose it. That means that you can choose a different situation if you so desire.

There is so much money floating around in this world yet there are so many people struggling without. It is because most of us don't think correctly in terms of finances. Finances are rarely taught in school. Mama and daddy didn't teach us because they weren't taught. Our basic lessons were to save some money for a rainy day. That's not teaching you a lot. How many times have you heard the saying "the rich get richer and the poor get poorer"? It is true and it is written in the bible. Yes, God says that it will continue to happen that way. If you don't understand finances and the economy tanks, you will suffer. If you do understand finances and the economy tanks, you will probably prosper. You don't have to trade time for money as most people do. You can invest your time so that you will gain money long after the investment of your time has ended. That is one-way people with a different way of thinking gain wealth.

What does "afford" mean to you? Think about it for a minute. Can you really afford a $30k-$50k car because you have the money to meet the payments every month? We put so much stock into our pleasures; the things that we just want to have, not need. What about the concept of "seed wheat"? You can't eat all of your crops. You need to save some seeds for next year's crop. We spend everything we make instead of keeping some back and planting it somewhere to grow a new crop of cash. I urge you to do something if you are having financial issues. It is really simple. Read a couple of books and apply the principles. There are principles that can change our situation if we learn them and apply knowledge. It is such a small investment.

Money problems act as an accelerant on other problems and issues in our lives. Relationship issues, job issues, and health issues are compounded when you mix in your financial problems. It is the gasoline on the fire. No matter how much you try to hide it and no matter how you try to mask it with more and more stuff, others see your financial strain. Money problems take precedence over most other issues. You might as well get a hold of that situation and learn to eliminate money as being a controlling factor in your life. The leading cause of divorce is money. The number one reason for incarceration in America has to do with money. People are hungry, sick, and dying because of the lack of money. Surprisingly, it's not the lack of making money; it's the lack of financial wisdom. Money management is just as important or more than knowing how to make money. No one should be broke December 26th, but so many people will be well beyond financially insolvent the day after Christmas. I guess it's okay because we can buy that temporary happiness for our children, spouses and loved ones. The Jones' get to try and keep up with us for once. So what if we have to eat peanut butter and jelly sandwiches or bologna until March. We can pay everything off and catch up on all of the bills when the tax refund check gets here.

I know you think you deserve all of the new technologies that are coming out -- that nice new car, and all of those designer outfits. Maybe your children deserve the best presents and gifts that are out right now. If you haven't worked to build a substantial income, managed well, and saved a good portion of your earnings, or haven't been living within your means, you don't deserve it. You and your family don't deserve to fall deeper into financial turmoil because of the commercialization of Christmas. Do the things that are necessary to ensure your family's financial security. I'm not saying be a Scrooge! Find a balance. Find a way to really enjoy the Holidays without tapping too deep into your resources that are supposed to build your financial freedoms versus take them away.

If no one in my neighborhood drove a new car or at my job or at church or that I went to school with, I wouldn't want one. I wouldn't need one. It is amazing how we can do without when no one else has it. But as soon as others start coming around with their new "this" or the latest "that", we just have to have it as well.

The advertisers know exactly what they are doing. They're coming after you hard. If they can't get you directly, they will come at you through their not-so-secret weapon, your friends and peers. They know that someone will cave. Keeping up with the Jones' is an American national pastime. That's not the game you want to play. The Jones' are going broke and we follow as if broke is normal. It's most Americans' new normal. Mr. and Mrs. Jones live life spending every bit of money they have, they buy the best the world has to offer, and most of it doesn't truly belong to them because they finance everything. I know a young man whose name happens to be Jones. Of course he was playing devil's advocate when he stated that you are not promised tomorrow. You should enjoy all the better things of life; spend all of your money 'cause you can't take nothing to the grave. The problem is this. What if you do live to a ripe old age and you have squandered all of your talents in your youth. You will be living your golden years crammed into a small apartment making tomato soup out of ketchup and hot water.

We are programmed by advertisers to give them the money we have worked hard for on items we really don't need. They are going to use others to make you want those things. We have to learn to control the information that is coming into our heads. Do you think that your body naturally craves Mountain Dew or Diet Coke? No, it may be thirsty and you need something to drink. When you crave specific brands of food, beverages and even non-consumable products, it is the result of someone tapping into your mind and dictating your desires. It is a tough battle, but one you must fight. There are always conflicts and fights when it comes to money.

My heart finally stopped racing and my mind settled down as I drove home last night. I was in a bidding war with several people and even more so, I was in a war with myself. My family and I were at the annual Fall Festival of my son's elementary school. There were games, prizes, food and fun. Inside of the gymnasium was a silent auction of art, dinner certificates, jewelry and much more. Back and forth I bid on items. There was competition among many people, bidding and re-bidding, trying to outdo the next person. I must have signed my name and increased bids on six or seven items. I won four and was happy to pay. Each one was a great deal. Silent auctions usually are a great place for scoring great deals and the money benefits great causes.

By the time I got home, I couldn't believe that I had spent so much money on items I didn't need. My new financial intelligence teaches me to avoid emotional spending, yet I fell into that trap. It was a self-induced trap. I have no problem with the amount of money I spent. I have a problem with the lack of control and discipline that I displayed. I now recognize that I had lost control. It was as if I had no choice. We always have a choice. My emotions were in control of my wallet. Good deals ruin our financial discipline. We believe everything is a good deal and we can't let a good deal go. Do I really need a certificate for two chiropractic consultations including x-rays?

The price was too low not to bid. I placed a bid on a framed Pati Bannister print, and I'm not a fan of her paintings at all. I even made bids on items my wife made bids on. She didn't need them but I was driven by emotions to win those items for her that she got outbid on.

It's okay to be spontaneous at times with your spending. It's okay to treat yourself to things you don't need or buy something for a loved one. It's not okay to let your emotions get out of control and regret what you have done later. When it comes to spending money, we need to sleep on a lot of our decisions. We need to evoke a twenty-four hour rule. Come up with a number that you are comfortable with spending. Maybe your number is $50, $100, or whatever. No matter what, you should never spend over that amount of money without allowing yourself 24 hours to think about the decision to spend that money. That allows you to detach yourself from the emotional tie of the good deal. You may come back and get the item and that's okay. You may think on it and decide that you really don't need it. How many of us have bought things that we really don't need, only to realize it later and feel bad about it?

Sometimes we get so involved emotionally with sales and bargains that we purchase items that we already have. All we see is how low the price is and we get home to discover that we already have one or we never use the items. Get your emotions in check when it comes to your finances and protecting your future wealth. Control your emotions and watch your wealth grow.

I recently had a conversation with an old friend from high school. Years ago, I took him under my wing. I tried to teach him some sound principles that would hopefully carry him through the next few years because I would be gone and he would need them to survive. He was just a freshman during my senior year, but I knew he needed the information I had because he would one day be in my shoes. He expressed some of the things that I shared with him and never forgot. I was humbled at the fact that he told me that he was still following me through the teachings I share every day. He was concerned about me over-emphasizing money and finances.

In my life I try to teach on every aspect of this world that I feel others need guidance in, through my own experiences and learning. One thing I have realized is that if we can solve the problems in our financial situations, most other issues will subside. By no means do I teach materialism. I teach wealth through knowledge and wisdom. On my path of a Self-directed Shift, I discovered that financial security equals freedom.

What is freedom? Most people believe that they are free, but truly are not because of their financial situation. Freedom equals choices. The fewer the choices you have, the less free you are. The more money you have, the more choices and the more freedom. You are not free to do much when you are broke. That is the world we live in. In some cases, freedom (money) determines whether you live or die. This is sad but true. The rich live longer because they have the freedom to eat healthier and make better choices. If a bunch of bananas cost $3.50 and a whopper cost $.99, which choice do you think the poor person will make? We all know which is healthier and the better choice, but your freedom often makes you choose the cheap unhealthy-but-filling foods in the grocery store, versus the nutritious life-sustaining and life-saving whole foods. Where would you like to go in this world? Many have dreams of traveling the globe to see exotic places but never will because they will never gain that freedom. It takes money. Freedom is bought. Most people I know are enslaved. I am enslaved. To what degree are you free? It is to the degree of your choices, which are determined by your bank account. I hear all of the time from people that money isn't everything or that they don't care about money. Money is behind everything and when you don't have it, you have to get it from somewhere or someone who does.

May I borrow some of your FREEDOM? Will you give me some of your FREEDOM? Maybe I will take your FREEDOM at gunpoint! You have to get your own freedom. Freedom is attained through information and understanding on how money works, how to attract it, how to make it work, and how to keep it in your possession. How much FREEDOM do you want?

Money is the root of all evil. Have you heard that somewhere before? I hope you don't believe it. That is one of the most misquoted verses in the bible. For the love of money is the root of all sorts of evil. That's more like it, depending on your particular version of the bible. Money is not good or evil, but money is very important to you and me because of the way society is set up. If you don't rank it up there with oxygen you will never have a lot of it. It is a tool that provides us with food, shelter, entertainment, education and so much more. Earle Nightingale states, "Money is the harvest of our production. Money is what we receive for our production and service as persons which we can then use to obtain the production and services of others."

Don't be fooled when you hear someone say that money doesn't buy happiness. If you are broke, out of work, and don't know where your next meal will come from, I'll bet you would be pretty happy if I stuck a hundred-dollar bill in your hand. The more money you have, the more freedom you will possess. Yes, money relates to freedom. Without money you are limited in our society, or you become dependent on those with money to provide you with freedoms. We move about this earth depending upon the dead presidents in our pockets. You are not even free to live as long as you physically can without money. Wealthy people live longer because money buys them the freedom to eat healthier, live in better environmental conditions, and for the most part are free from the deadliest killer known to man -- Stress. Millions of people have stress levels that soar through the roof every month when the bills are due. Compound that over twenty or thirty years and just like that, slow singing and flower bringing. Find your value. Figure out a way to eliminate the money issue. Find your freedom. That doctor you visit, the lawyer in the courtroom, and the businessman you see with a house on the beach are not better than you. They may just have more value than you. If you don't like the amount of money you are making, go out and make more. Your money will come from your service and value. Solve problems, create jobs, do something new or do something different. People are doing it everyday. Even in this bad economy there is tons of money waiting on you. I've provided services to people my whole life and I suspect that I always will. I connect the dots. I find a need and I fill the void because there are certain freedoms that I know come with having money. Is not fair that someone your same age, gender, IQ level, education level, born in the same area, and had the same opportunity, has more freedom than you?

A few days ago, I lectured to a group of teenagers in a personal finance class and I was very pleased with their attentiveness and focus on the topic of finances and money matters. It's funny how easy it is to get teens to pay attention when you teach subjects with plenty of relevance in their lives. The truth is, money matters in this world. When you master or begin to truly understand how money works and how life works in relationship to monetary principles, everything in life goes better.

Money issues cause problems everywhere. Master money and you can master anything; but mastering money is not easy. It is simple but not easy. Your relationships, jobs, and health usually become better when money is not an issue or when you are not a slave to the money. It is very important to make a self-directed shift into learning finances. Years ago I couldn't talk on the subject. My financial situation was horrible despite the fact that I had a good job and was part of a two-income household. I just didn't have the right information circulating in my brain. I can talk on many money issues, but the one I wish to share now is saving.

Just about my whole life, the only financial advice I was given was to save money. I believe in it but I'm not 100% for saving money as in the traditional sense of saving for tomorrow. Our grandparents saved 10% of what they made and they lived on that when they retired. That's not working today. People are living longer and the money is being deflated like a tire stabbed with a butcher's knife. In 1971 we were taken off of the gold standard. Prior to that, each dollar was backed by a piece of gold. Today a dollar is just a piece of paper, and that piece of paper will be worth less tomorrow than it is today.

Think about this. Twenty years ago you could have put $20 of gas in your car and got a full tank. Let's say you put that twenty-dollar bill in the bank and pulled it out today. How much gas would it buy? Certainly, it would not buy a full tank. Maybe it could get half or a quarter of a tank. Your money is worth less over time. Sure, there is interest that occurs, but interest doesn't outrun inflation. I believe that you should save to a certain degree. Save enough for an emergency. Save enough so that you can get out of a bind or have the capital to do the things that increase the quality of your life.

So, it is good to save, but it is more important to invest in assets and create a cash flow. You need money that is constantly flowing into your wallet. Sure, you have a job that is doing that, but you can't work forever or you shouldn't work forever. Most people get retirement jobs. They have to work after they retire because the money isn't enough. There are ways to create a constant stream of money and there are things you can invest in that appreciate in value. I know a person with two businesses that does not use banks to save money. He buys Rolex watches and other valuable things with the money that most people would save by sticking it in the bank. When he needs large lumps of money, he sells a watch or some other commodity that appreciates in value like gold. Why do you see so many signs that read "we buy gold"? There are certain things that will rise in value over time. Your money, that paper dollar, will depreciate over time. That $20 dollar bill you save for a year, will look like $20 dollars but will only spend like it's $18 dollars. When you earn money or receive money, it has the value of that day. The longer you hold it, the less it is worth and the fewer things it can purchase. Your money shouldn't be sitting in a bank gaining you interest that is slower than the rate of inflation. Your money should be working for you making you more money. Banks and financial institutions are doing just that. They are taking your money and putting it to work. They make six bucks off of your dollar and give you a few cents. You really don't need someone else making your money work for them and then giving you table scraps.

Saving money is just one thing we need to understand a little better. There are others that are equally important. I recommend that you start a self-directed education on finance and create a Self-directed Shift in your awareness and growth. I recommend diving into financial books and a great DVD from Robert Kiyosaki's "Sacred Cows". I recently found a set of Financial CDs in a local Goodwill store for only $3.00. It was one of my best investments. I am amazed at how much financial information there is out there that can transform the lives of so many people. With the Internet and YouTube, we are information-rich but wisdom-poor because we won't use the information to save our lives.

Most people wouldn't see the value in that $3.00 set of CDs that actually retail for over $100.00. We are not willing to pay what it will take to get us out of our financial hole.

I've been "hustling" for as long as I can remember. I sold powdered Kool-Aid, blow-pops and ink pens way back in the third grade. I've done a number of things to get ahead in life. I have friends that admire my hustle and complain to me that they don't have a "hustle". In great economic times, I do well. In poor economic times, I do great. During the Great Depression there were individuals who did well for themselves. There is always money to be made because money will always be spent. Your pride may get in the way of you attaining those dollars, but they are out there.

It hurts me to hear people complain about being broke and they aren't doing anything about it. Here's my concept. Find out what your friends are spending their money on and provide that service for them. Provide the same or better value for less than what they would otherwise pay. The chances are high that your pride won't allow you to make a few extra dollars in your hard times. I got over that. It does not bother me, how others look at me for doing jobs that are common but may seem to be below my pay grade. I have no problem with washing your car or shining your shoes. You have talents that can get you over the hump as long as you get over your pride. You can bake cakes and pies, sell dinner plates, watch a neighbor's kids, clean someone's house, or provide laundry services. People are going to spend money for the things they want and need whether the economy is up or down. You just have to figure out and provide the services or products that they desire. Maybe that's beneath you. Well, maybe you really are okay with being broke.

A friend of mine said, "I didn't know you do graduation announcements". I laughed and thought, "What don't I do!" I tell my friends to check with me before they do anything. I may be able to provide that service. Think of all of your talents and gifts. What can you do to earn extra money? I know that the job you get a check for is not the only way you can make money. If you can provide services or products that save me money, I'm all for that. What if we traded talents so that neither of us had to spend money? When I was sixteen, I turned my 1975 Cadillac into a taxi. It was five dollars for a ride just about anywhere. You have a "hustle" in you. Find it. Back in the day, everyone had a "hustle". That's how our communities survived. We had the freeze-cup lady, the shade tree mechanic, the barbers and beauticians. None of these were their "real" jobs. They were hustling. Back in school I knew a girl who starched jeans for $5. One of my classmates sold eggrolls out of her book bag. She still does today and she has a good government job.

Put your gifts and talents to work. Stop complaining about being broke. Humble yourself and put your pride to the side. Provide others with a service that will help you get through these hard times. Most people will understand that you are honest and just trying to make it. Who knows, your hustle may become your passion and your passion may become your new career.

How much did you pay for that new car you purchased? What about those shoes on your feet or that nice outfit you're wearing? They weren't free. There was definitely a cost. You wouldn't be driving or wearing those threads if you didn't pay for them. Maybe you didn't pay the price, but someone had to. Success can be broken into these simple things: You must decide what it is you want, figure out what it costs, and pay for it. Those with little or no success in life tend to miss the boat in one of these areas. Some just get what life throws their way because they never figure out what they want. They never set their eyes on a prize. Through some strange set of events, they have convinced themselves that they really don't want much out of life. They struggle from day to day, yet tell themselves that their life is good. It could be fancy cars or a big house, but I'm not just talking about material possessions. What you really want or need may be a healthy relationship or being in good physical shape. You have to want or desire something to get it. If you want nothing, then nothing you will receive. Others want lots of things or they may get fixated on one particular object or desire and never get it because they haven't figured out what it costs to have it.

Imagine walking into a store full of running shoes. You want running shoes and you are in the right place. You lift and turn over almost every shoe but find no price tag. In your frustration, you leave the store and have to continue running on those same old running shoes you've had for years. A few simple steps of finding a clerk and finding out how much they cost could have saved your frustration. Next would be the largest group of people out there. They know what they want and they know the cost, but they are not willing to pay the price. "I'll wait until they go on sale." Unlike those Nike, Reebok or Adidas, success never goes on sale. There is a cost and a price to pay. There is no negotiating or haggling. There is no discount super store for success. Wal-Mart does not carry success in a box. Decide what you want, find out the cost, and pay it. This is a really simple process. What you want may be very expensive so you're going to have to work very hard to pay for it.

It was my birthday and I got many gifts. Those gifts were the well wishes of family and friends through phone calls, text messages and messages on social media. I bought myself one special gift on that day that didn't cost very much but was worth 100x more than what I paid for it. First, I picked my sons up after school and took them with me to the bookstore. They ran around in the kid's section as I purchased the book that I had reserved earlier in the day. Landon, my oldest, asked me, "What book did you buy?" I told him that we would talk about it later. Next, we went to the bank and drove through its drive-thru. Landon then asked, "Does the bank pay you to keep your money there?" Good question from an eight-year-old. I then smiled and showed him the book I had just purchased. It is by Robert T. Kiyosaki, a financial author and one of the leading experts on finances. The book is called: *Why "A" STUDENTS Work for "C" STUDENTS and "B" STUDENTS work for the government. Rich Dad's Guide to Financial Education for Parents.* "How to give your child a financial head start without giving them money."

I started my Self-directed Shift later in life and have struggled from the lack of financial knowledge. I am determined to give my children, among many things, the financial principles and education to help them avoid the pitfalls and financial burdens that plague most Americans. When you start educating yourself and start to ascend due to a Self-directed Shift, encourage someone else to step out of line. Why not encourage your children? Start them on a shift by teaching them principles and more importantly teaching them to teach themselves, because we won't always be there to ensure their success. They are never too young for you to start feeding them good information in dealing with money.

Kiyosaki's book is so fascinating that my first read was 42 pages and I had to force myself to stop reading. I am fortunate to have great mentors in my work, business and personal life who act as beacons of light to guide me in the directions that I wish to follow.

The separation between poor or average people and the wealthy is information. That information leads to choices and subsequently to our actions and results. If you want the life of the average, do what the average do. If you want the life of the wealthy, do what the wealthy do. You will never hear of the wealthy making statements like money is the root of all evil. Only people who think poorly say those kinds of things. There is an intentional relentlessness towards mastering money principles you must embrace. Formal education is a plus, but you don't have to be educated at an Ivy League school to master money and become good with it. It can be done through specific intentional direction on your own or through a mentor. It is a Self-directed Shift that starts with a self-directed education on finances. You must live below your means and stay away from emotional triggers. Look to the future versus instant gratification. Follow your passions and purpose. Don't just work to earn money. Do what it is you love. Set the bar high on what you are willing to do and willing to accept. You don't need money to make money. You only need drive and determination. Use other people's money when you don't have the capital of your own. There are plenty of people who don't have your ideas but have the dollars to help you build your dreams. You only need to find them. Constantly work on yourself. Invest in your brain. It pays the best dividends. Start your Self-directed Shift.

Over the past decade, I've witnessed Rickey's growth in the area of financial literacy through our many conversations and through my observation of his actions. He has developed a true passion for gaining knowledge of finances and wealth building strategies, but unlike most, he's just as passionate in teaching what he has learned to others. Grasping the subject requires a commitment and discipline that most are not willing to endure to achieve. The knowledge and information to improve your financial situation are plentiful-just walk down the "Self-Help" aisle of any bookstore or Google the topic. The prize comes to those who remain dedicated long-term to learning and implementing the principles shared within this chapter. This body of work is foundational in the search of financial freedom.

Jason Roberts

Sales and Investments Advisor,

State Farm Insurance Co.

CHAPTER 9

Relational Beings

"It is the individual who is not interested in his fellow men who has the greatest difficulties in life and provides the greatest injury to others."

-Dale Carnegie

How are you with people? Would others say you are a people person? You don't have to be the life of the party or a social butterfly, but you do need to develop your relationships with others and increase your interpersonal skills. We need each other. Yes, we are relational beings who thrive or fail based on the effective connectivity with others. The explosion of social media is a result of our need to belong and connect to others. We might as well connect in positive ways and learn to deal with others that ultimately result in the benefit of all. We don't just need to become effective in our relationships with friends, family and acquaintants. We need to be able to deal with everyday people who come in and out of our lives as we move about this world. We are constantly crossing the paths of people from every walk of life. They are dependent on us and we are dependent on them and most of us don't even think about it. Think about how many people you are dependent on in just one single day of your life. Imagine if you were the only person on earth but you still had to do all of the things you normally do. How many objectives could you accomplish entirely by yourself? Not many. You need the butcher, the baker and the candlestick maker.

No one person can win at this game of life by himself. I need you and whether you admit it or not, you need me. Maybe not me personally, but you need someone else to help you along your path to a great life. We are born dependent on others to survive. Some animals on this planet are born and need no help to survive. You and I are different. It is part of human nature. I can't stress it enough. We need each other. Being independently strong is a good concept. It builds and embodies confidence in ourselves, but no one can succeed alone. Think back on your life to all of the things that you worked really hard at and accomplished. You have done great things so far and seemingly you pulled yourself up by the bootstraps and made it happen with your own effort. Now, take away all of the human connectivity to those tasks and ask yourself the question, " Could I have really done that completely by myself?" If your answer is yes to any big success, I suggest you take a lesson in humility. Every success of your life is tied to the previous successes, which are held together by others lending support in some shape, form or fashion.

I could not have been drafted into professional baseball without the help of my college teammates or coaches. The college scholarship would not have been possible without my high school coaches, teacher support, or friends and family. I couldn't imagine if my mother would not have signed me up for that first t-ball season when I was six. Every success, every major accomplishment, and everything that I am proud to say I've accomplished, has come from an interlocking web of others doing just the right things at just the right times. When you understand that, you become a part of the web for others. Not all people have grabbed onto that concept yet. They don't think they need anyone and they believe that all that they have is by their works alone. Those are self-centered people who can't seem to gain much ground no matter how hard they work. Most of their success is superficial.

There's a formula that works in life through the powers of the universe. If you help enough people get what they want out of life, you can get everything you want out of life. Focus on others. Serve the next person. Give up your comfort so that the next guy may have comfort. There is always sacrifice connected to success. We may not even be the one who had to sacrifice when we gained the success. Someone sacrificed for you. It may have been many years prior to your success and you may not even know who sacrificed themselves for you. Be proud of yourself and let's be proud of each other. Thank your mother, thank a friend, thank a teacher or someone who has helped you accomplish successes in your life where you previously thought that your successes were solely of your own doing. Thank God for all of the successes he made possible in your life. Thank your friends for having your back through the tough times.

Do you have any friends? So you have a lot of friends on social media websites! Are you proud of that fact? I know I was as I started really getting into online communities. I couldn't believe it when I started getting Friend Requests, when I hit 500 friends, when someone would "like" one of my photographs or one of my comments, and when out of the blue, I would get notices that so-and-so is now following me. It does feel good. It is a boost to your ego. I can only imagine how one feels who is socially out of place in real communities but now has hundreds of friends in these pseudo communities. They have a voice. They can express themselves and don't have to hide from their social anxiety.

The question is this. How many of your hundreds of friends can you invite to your home for dinner? How many would you! We go back and forth conversing with one another. How many of our online friends would we go meet on the side of the road if they posted that they had a flat tire? Darlene Jones said something in a conversation we had one day that has stuck to me. We know longer call Sycamore and St. Francis (insert the streets where you live if it applies) the neighborhood. We just call it "The Hood". The neighbor has been dropped from our social consciousness. Are you neighborly? When was the last time you borrowed a cup of sugar? When was the last time you baked a pie for the new couple who has moved into the neighborhood? Do we even visit with those across the street?

Can your neighbor correct your child for misbehaving in the streets? I think not. The community has moved into the cyber world. We don't have to look at each other's faces and see the pain and struggle. We look at that profile picture that has a permanent smile that says "I'm doing great". How can you hug that person who just lost a family member? You can only type your emotions through the keys. There are little square buttons that we give the task of spelling out emotions that are meant to be expressed through face-to-face contact. We are definitely relational beings. We need to belong. We need each other but we are losing so much of our humanity via the social media. In no way am I against social networking and connecting to others through the web. I just feel that we need to reconnect to the world. We need to reconnect ourselves to each other. The real communities are being broken down, dismantled, and pushed away for these new artificial neighborhoods formed on the streets of the World Wide Web. We need to make more real connections and start leaning on one another to help us grow. In our growth we must learn to be true friends. Clicking a button does not make true friends.

Do you have a true friend? Great and successful relationships are based on two people being the best they can be and inspiring the other to be the best they can be. A true friend will inspire you to be the best person you can become and helps you find and fulfill your purpose. Are you doing that to the person you consider your best friend? Are you inspiring any of your friends to be all that they can be? Do you just accept them when they decide to do less than what they are capable of or what they should be doing?

Friends come in and out of our lives. Some friends are only around for a season and others are around for a lifetime. It's always difficult when we lose a friend for whatever reason. I have friends from coast to coast that many I may never see again. What impact did I leave on their life? Does it even matter? It does matter because their impact on you matters. We are built by the relationships that we have in our lives and the ones formed through years of interacting with others. What are you getting from those around you? What are you giving?

We may not admit it, but we act differently around different people. Are we being the best person we can be and are we bringing out the best in others? We must see past others' faults and into their gifts and talents that we can encourage. Let's find the good in our friends and stop focusing on their shortcomings. We all need to grow. Grown implies that we are finished growing. You're finished growing when you're in the grave. I'm not grown. Friends should be challenging each other to grow and be the best person they can be. Listen when they talk. Really listen! Sometimes the words coming out of their mouth doesn't match what they are saying. They may need help but don't know how to say it. We have to listen so that we can hear what is in their heart.

False friends are like shadows keeping close to us while we walk in the sunshine but leaving us when we cross into the shade. A real friend sticks with us when trouble comes. -John Maxwell

All of us have a frame of reference, which makes up our worldview. The way people act is in direct relationship to the way they view the world. In dealing with people, it is much easier to try to understand their view rather than trying to make others understand our view. We must try to enter their world to understand them. A lot of the turmoil between people is because we can't see from someone else's perspective. We need to put ourselves in their shoes. It's a difficult task but necessary to build relationships. That world view that you possess and that others possess has been built since birth from emotional reactions to certain events and relationships in their lives. Many viewpoints from certain people are blurred and out of focus because of the environmental filter that they have seen the world in, has been skewed.

I had to stop judging people by their actions and thoughts because they are different from mine. Those who I would shake my head at were just acting and reacting in ways that reflect their worldview. It is the way they see things because of the life they have lived. We look down on others who we believe are acting inappropriately when they feel as if they are acting completely normal. We must enter their world so that we can relate to them in order to show them that what they perceive as reality may not be so. By simply pulling on others to see from your viewpoint causes conflict and resentment. I've pulled and pulled at some and caused more damage than good. No one wants to be told that they are wrong. I certainly didn't. It is much better to discover that your worldview is off center on your own.

How do we help others discover that they may be looking at the picture upside down? Very carefully! First we must understand their worldview so that you can comprehend and interpret that person's behavior, actions and thought processes. In dealing with people more and more each day, I have to really do a good job of getting into their shoes. Gaining that perspective of others often shows a person's self view as well. It is the image that they have of themselves which has been formed from years of environmental influences. I see and counsel many people with a poor worldview and an even poorer self-view. It is possible to help people change their view, but it is a slow process. Often frustrating to me because I want to help. I think I have come to a point where I can enter a person's world and be empathetic to their view because I am learning and understanding perspective.

The next time you criticize a person for their actions, remember this. They didn't grow up the exact way you did. They may have had some situations that tainted their opinions. Life may have been a little nicer to you or maybe they have had a series of struggles that won't allow them to see as you see. Your worldview is only yours. Two feet to the left or the right can make the picture completely different. Understanding others is a part of the Self-directed Shift, which propels us to better personal relationships.

As you move further down the success track and higher on the self-directed shift, you grow further away from many people who you used to have similar thinking with. You are growing further away from your former self. It is an awesome feeling, discovery. There's nothing like "figuring it out". There are many answers that are coming to you, that are leading you out of darkness and into the light. You wish that you could put every bit of knowledge that you have gained into others' heads. Part of the growth process is knowing that everyone has the ability but knowing that not everyone will grow and succeed. Many will be left behind and you have to be okay with that.

It may be your best friend, your mother, or even your children. With that said, we must not alienate ourselves from those we care for because they don't get it. You were once in that same position. I see people who have changed their lives for the better, and continuously condemn those who do the same things that they themselves used to do.

Early in my journey, I couldn't see why others were so blind. I would get upset and call people stupid because the curtain was still covering their eyes. I would explain, "if you do x, y, and z, then everything will change". They would continue doing what they have been doing their whole life and they continue getting the same results. It bothered me that I had answers to problems that some were complaining about and they wouldn't even make an effort to change. They've been in misery for so long that it's normal. It hurts bad enough to complain but not bad enough to do anything about it. I've realized it and you're going to have to realize it. This is the way the world works.

It's natural for small groups to gain all of the successes in life over the majority. In comparison to the over three hundred million people in the U.S., there are only a small percentage of people making the majority of the money, physically fit, have great relationships, love their jobs, have true freedom, and are genuinely overall happy with their lives. As you master every category of your life, don't look down at those who do not. They live in that normality. Success and excellence is an abnormality. You are moving into a class of people that is rare. Others can join you at any point. They just have to decide to break free from the pack. Encourage others to grow as you continue to develop a strong faith, master your financial situation, become healthy and fit, establish and grow great relationships and become a leader. As we grow and become persons of character, integrity, masters of our world, and purpose-driven, know that only a few will climb that ladder with you. Not every student will graduate; not every male will become a man; not everyone will get to know God; and not everyone will experience the successes that life has to offer. We just have to love them where they are.

Let me tell you about the time I saved my dog. Well, he isn't exactly my dog. He was my neighbor's dog, who happen to be my father-in-law. We share a large piece of property where the dog named Peanut runs freely from his house to mine. I feed him from time to time when he greets me at the driveway of my home. Some time ago we all went on a family trip for about a week and when we returned, there was no Peanut, who is a Labrador and Pit Bull mix. For the next three weeks there was no sign of him until one late night about five miles away from home I drove past what seemed to be Peanut. I backed up and sure enough it was Peanut.

He was filthy, nasty and had lost a lot of weight. I was afraid to approach him because of the fear of what he appeared to have become. He was responsive to his name so that let me know that the good ol' dog that I once knew was still in there. He would not let me pick him up and put him in the car, but he did follow me as I drove slowly for five miles. He was willing to follow me home but not as fast as I would have liked. Imagine traveling about 5-6 mph, late at night, down a dark and lonely road leading your dog home. I had to keep encouraging him because it seemed as if he was too exhausted to go on. I wouldn't let him stop because I knew what was waiting for him if he made it back. We made it home in about an hour, I fed him, gave him water and he collapsed at the foot of our garage with a look of relief.

He was home, safe and ready to put the past behind him. He fattened back up and life for this dog is back to great. I often think " What if I hadn't saw him or helped him home? What would have become of Peanut?' We all have our "dogs", those friends and family that are lost out there, waiting for us to drive by. They are desperately hoping you stop. They may not get in the car with you, but they will follow at a pace that's just their speed if you continue to encourage them to come home. Don't be afraid of what you think they have become. See if they need a ride. Maybe you're that dog, trapped inside of addictions, feelings of loneliness, depression, or maybe you just can't find your way home. Have faith; your ride is coming. Don't be afraid to bark. Let your presence in the darkness be known. Call on that friend that you know will be there to pick you up. There's a better life waiting for you if you can just make it back home. We may just need to encourage and edify them.

Edification is bringing out the best in others. It is finding the positive in people and verbally pointing it out to them and others. It is focusing on a person's strong qualities and good traits. Too often we do the opposite. I was good at that. We took time tearing each other down when I was in school. We called it "janking". You may know it as "playing the dozens". At the time it was great. It was in good fun. I knew in my heart that some people were really hurt, but I just had to get that next laugh. Nowadays people shy away from those who constantly pick at others even if they are joking and meaning no harm. The fact is that there is harm. We have too much negativity in our world that people trying to make it have to deal with. Try edifying those around you. Look for the best in them. Tell them what a great job they're doing. Be sincere and thankful for their service to you and others. Lift others up and make them feel good. It will boomerang back to you and make you feel good. Start searching for the good in people you come in contact with. Don't worry about the bad or poor qualities. When you point out those things, the person will fire back with negativity or just get defensive. Edify them and they will continue to work on improving and always look forward to your presence.

Name a person who has not done anything good in life. There is no such person created by God. We may have to search really hard in some people, but everyone has some good qualities and good achievements in their life. Be sincere. It may take some time to build your thinking towards searching for the good in others. Compliment a person on having a good smile, how hard they work, the way they are always thinking of others, or how great they do in tough situations. Edification can be done indirectly. Talk positively about people to others. It will get back to them. Gossip great things, not the bad.

People are looking for someone to praise the good that they do. They need to know that others notice their work, their effort and their positive traits. They have been told about the negative or not-so-good things they do all of their life. Practice edification today. Be a good finder and verbally express that good you see in others.

You can close your eyes if you want to, but the problem is not just going to disappear. At some point you will have to open them and the issue will be staring you in the face. We often believe that if we don't talk about it, it will just go away. We believe that if we can't see an issue right in our face, it doesn't exist. If we turn our heads and squint our eyes, it will somehow go away. Ignoring an issue doesn't make it go away. Avoidance usually leads to the problem getting bigger. Take your vehicle for example. You may hear the brakes make a slight little squeak. You can ignore it, but over time you will have to change your brakes. The sound will become unbearable because the problem, left untreated, will only get worse.

We must become problem solvers and not problem avoiders. Especially when problems involve other people. Conflict resolution is one of the toughest of human issues to deal with. Most of us are not equipped with the necessary skills of mastering conflicts with others. That is why so many friendships are thrown away. Being a teacher, I watch teens go from their freshman year to their senior year with several different sets of friends and best friends. Problems arise. It is part of our human nature. They avoid solving the issue or they don't know how to effectively resolve the conflict, so they simply stop being friends. They move on. It's not just kids outgrowing their friends. They lack the resolution skill set. It's not just the youth. Adults do the same thing. What if you were leaving your house and you glanced at the kitchen sink filled with water and dirty dishes? The faucet is not quite off and it has a little drip. There is a problem that needs to be addressed. It may take a small amount of effort to unplug the sink or clean the dishes and turn off the faucet. What if you ignored it and were gone for hours that day. The problem will definitely have gotten worse. The sink is sure to fill and overflow causing a mess, which will take considerably more work to rectify.

Between stimulus and response is choice. We choose our actions but we also choose our feeling. We must guard our thoughts and feelings from being reactive. I used this example with my students a few days ago: If I spit on you, what would you be? One young lady said that she would be mad and would slap me. I told her "No, you would be wet. You would choose to be mad at me. If I hand you a new born baby and that baby spit on you, would you be mad? " Her answer was no because it's a baby and it doesn't know any better. The fact is, in that situation you would have chosen your feelings differently from the same two stimuli.

Once we understand that there is choice in between stimulus and response, even in that fraction of a second, we can create a more meaningful life that puts us on a better path.

Animals are reactive. Oftentimes you hear people refer to others as "acting like animals". That's especially in situations concerning violence. The only difference between animals and humans are our minds and our power of choice. If you take away your choice and simply allow yourself to react without thought, you have joined the animal kingdom. Stop and think about what has happened to you, what someone has said to you, or what kind of reaction you are about to have.

Stephen R. Covey says to hit the pause button. Some say count to ten or take deep breaths. It is our human ability to stop and choose. I know it is hard at first, because we see reactions as natural and uncontrollable. Reacting has gotten me in much trouble over the years. Newton's law of relativity states, for every action there is an equal and opposite reaction. The law doesn't explain the existence in the humanity of choice. Today choose to be responsible. Be a responsible person. "Response-able" means: able to choose your response.

Many conflicts start off as small little seemingly insignificant hiccups, but they grow and get out of control. Problems are going to occur from time to time. We can't avoid them and we must learn how to successfully deal with them as they show up in our lives. We need to stop what we are doing and address the problem. At least shut the faucet off. What if it's not the sink but it's the toilet. You better get the plunger and shut off the water, because who wants to deal with all of the crap that will hit the floor from that problem!

No matter how small you think the issue is, talk to them about it. Refuse to let it grow larger than what it already is. You have to get over the fear of confronting the conflict. We are often more fearful of the conflict than the results of the conflict. Value your friendship enough to solve the problem today. Tomorrow might be too late.

On social media I posted some wild and crazy things. I've had a following my entire life because of my tomfoolery. My life was changing because I was changing. I figured people would follow me like Moses when I started writing thought-provoking and meaningful messages. Not so. I really wasn't parting any seas or giving these messages on stone tablets. I was just reminding people of principles that are already out there, and that are already built inside each one of us.

With my love language being Words of Affirmation, I was somewhat disappointed in the amount of responses from a world that could use some encouragement and positive finger pointing. Soon that changed when people started sending me messages and calling on me for advice. I've been approached by people I barely know who thank me for posting words that somehow brighten their day that otherwise may have been gloomy. I've been stopped after church, and just the other day an old friend and former classmate shared some really good words about the change she sees in my life from the writings I post. I hadn't seen her in years and didn't realize that we were social media friends.

No matter if anyone clicks a Like button or posts a comment to my post, I know they are out there watching. People are watching you too. There are many ears and eyes in this world. They are all around us even when they don't make themselves appear. So much of what you do is being watched. What you say is being heard. Your actions will be copied, ridiculed, or dismissed as irrelevant. Remember that it will be seen whether you think so or not.

One day when I was nine years old, my sister and I were playing at the park across the street from the projects where we lived. A neighborhood kid, a couple of years older than me was pushing and shoving my sister and I did nothing. At that point in my life, I had the heart of the Cowardly Lion. I looked around, saw no one that could help, and did nothing. Later that night I found out that my sister's father watched the whole incident from afar in one of those project windows. Because I saw no one, I thought no one could see me. Have you ever played with a little toddler who puts their hands over their eyes and says, " You can't see me?" They truly believe that because they can't see you there that you can't see them. Don't be foolish to believe that what you are doing is not being seen. All of the good you do, all of the things you think are being overlooked, and your countless efforts to do right by others that you think aren't being seen, are being watched by many more than you think. No need to harp on the negative, but your slight errors in judgment are being watched as well by people you think don't even care or others who look up to you. Remember this and I hope it sticks!

There are some really important relationships that need cultivating. If you created a Self-directed Shift in only one area of your life, it should be with building the relationships of those closest to you. It may be husbands, wives, children, parents, or best friends.

One day you won't have to yell at your kids to clean their room. You won't have to have parent conferences with a teacher, follow the high school sports team out of town, or go listen to the band recital. The diapers will disappear. No longer will you have to punish them for making bad choices or being disobedient. The proms will come and go. The pictures will last but the moment of watching your little girl get pinned with a corsage will be gone. That little boy of yours won't need help learning to ride his bike without training wheels any longer. We yell at our kids to just grow up! One day they will. One day that house, their old room, and the yard they used to play in will be empty. Kids do grow up very fast. In an instant they can be playing with blocks and then buying and selling stocks. We can get so busy trying to provide for them and do the best we can for them that we don't really enjoy them for who they are today. Tomorrow they will be different. They will like different things. They are changing every day. Enjoy every one of their phases. Implant those memories into your brain of how they love to play tricks and sneak snacks from the pantry. Be a part of their memories. Do you know your children's favorite color? What are they really into? Their dreams change from time to time but, if asked today, what would they say they want to be when they grow up?

My wife got it right. There is nothing more precious to her than those three little boys who won't be little for long. She enjoys all of the good and the bad. We are building memories every day with each one of them. Are you building memories that will last forever? Are you cheating them because you are so busy? We must make time for our kids. They will only be kids once. I have to spend more time teaching them and just being in their presence. Often, I feel left out when I hear of the great adventure of the day or the one-liners from Landon, Lathan, and Larkin. All those things that may annoy you like crying for no reason, waking at the crack of dawn and sneaking out of the house will come to an end. And then what? How will you really feel? I know parents always say that they can't wait until their kids are out of the house, but will you really feel like that? Don't you wish you could keep them young forever? I can't imagine not hearing them fighting, turning up the television, or banging something against the wall. I can't imagine that silence.

I treated her like a king instead of the queen that she is. There are different roles that women and men must play according to the way God has built us and the way He wants us to function. There are certain roles and responsibilities that belong to each one of us that are proper in nature.

Before you get upset and curse, this is not some form of male chauvinism. I am not of the opinion that women should just cook, clean and take care of kids. I am of the opinion that the man is the head of the house. He is the leader and stronger vessel as designed by God. I gave my wife the crown. Mistakenly it was the wrong one. It was the one I should have been wearing. Probably because I watched my mother wear the King's Crown. My wife did an awesome job of holding our family together for years as I sat back and received the benefits of her labor and hard work. She carried the burdens that I should have carried: the stress of budgeting, managing, planning, disciplining, nurturing, and providing for us all. At times the load got really heavy for her and I was not there to lift it off of her back.

In Christ, males and females are equal; but in marriage, the husband is to assume the leadership. To be a leader you must serve. Husbands must serve their families as Christ served His people. Through the words of God, the man is responsible for his family's wellbeing. The woman can certainly provide everything that her family needs to survive, but it is not her responsibility.

Lauren and I went to Leon and Kari's wedding at the beautiful Oak Crest Mansion. There were many family members and friends in attendance. You could see that there was a lot of planning and thought that went into making this day, this wedding, a special one for the bride and groom as well as for all of the guests. I spoke to Leon at some point during the reception and we laughed and joked as we have done over the years, but I could not help but be overwhelmed with a feeling of wanting to talk to him on marriage from what I have studied and learned through experience and knocking my head against the wall. I didn't. It was not the time or the place. Perhaps I am not the one to counsel, but God and what he says in the bible about marriage could be counsel enough.

First of all, as men we are to love our wives as Christ loved the church. There is no greater love than that! Are you willing to die for your wife as Jesus died for His church? We ought to love our wives as we love our own bodies. We must take care of them as we take care of ourselves. The perspective of marriage today is so far from the establishment of marriage in the bible. We think we know what marriage is by today's standards, which have been skewed by movies and television. Your marriage probably shouldn't resemble any you see on television and maybe just a few you've ever witnessed. I know everyone who gets divorced does so for a number of reasons and there are times when it is the only option. Think about this though. Divorce is higher than it ever has been. The numbers are increasing and there doesn't seem to be any change coming in the future. Something has happened over time. It is tied to love.

Marriage today has gravitated to a very romantic version of love. It is more so, being in love and in a state of euphoria. Being in love has only been referenced in the bible about four times and three of those relationships did not last. Throughout the bible, love is referred to as an action, not a feeling. Today in our marriages we put the emphasis on the feelings. When those feelings fade, change, or they disappear; we think that the marriage is over. It is time to move on. No, it is time to move forward. It is time to start a new growth phase in marriage. We need a higher phase of prosperity that may not be tied to such a great degree of romantic love but a deeper more meaningful love. We need a selfless love, a devotional love, or perhaps a kind of love that can't be explained. We have to distance ourselves from the images and marriages portrayed in movies and romantic novels. We need to get back to the love that God intended for a man and a woman to have between them; back to a biblical marriage so that we stay together, work together, raise our children together and keep the bond that God made together. It's a lot of work to make it work in this world we live in. We put a lot of work into our weddings. We spend thousands and thousands of dollars on rings, tuxedos, dresses, banquet halls, food, cakes and honeymoons. Countless hours to make that one day, those few hours, as perfect as we can.

Why don't we put that much effort into making the marriage work? Why don't we invest a little money in a marriage therapist, good marriage books, or counsel with other married couples? That would create a Self-directed Shift in our marriage. Sometimes we do, but only when the point of no return seems to have been passed. You don't need to be on the brink of divorce to work on your marriage or any relationship as a matter of fact. Your situation may be great, but storms come. We should be prepared when they do. Sometimes we need to pack up and head to higher ground, but we need to pack up and seek shelter together!

In this age of independent women and the attitudes of not needing a man, it is hard for women to submit to men. So many of us men are not doing the things to warrant our women to follow us. They are taking the roles as king and doing without the man sometimes even when he's in the house. How many times have I heard, "I don't need a man."? Women, you do need a man. You can make it just fine without one, but you do need a man. God made us for each other. He created you for him and you need him just as much. This is a challenge to all of the men out there. Put a Queen's Crown on your woman's head and treat her like one. Provide for her. Put her on a pedestal. Serve her and your family as the king you are. Women, you are strong. You have proven this over and over. You've had to be because of the breakdown in the family structure. Give that man an opportunity to be King. Let him lead his family as God has instructed.

Our perspective and paradigms are different. I often do and say things that my wife doesn't understand or agree with. Many times, I don't have a clue as to why she feels the way she does, acts or reacts the way she does, or even says some of the things she says. It's not so much that we are different in personalities, philosophies or attitude as much as it is that we are male and female.

In our personal relationships we must understand that men see one way and women see another. We operate quite differently. If a good healthy relationship is what you desire, you need to learn and understand the difference. Men tend to focus linearly. For the most part we are one-tracked and find difficulty processing several tasks and conversations at once. We use logic and are often not keen to hints, suggestions and interpreting underlying meanings or agendas from our women. With that being said, we can learn those traits through intentionally focusing on improving our relationship.

Women naturally see, think and feel things all around them. They are processing information from 360 degrees, whereas men will process information from the front then turn to process the other information on the side after the first task is complete. If you put a male in a room with ten people having conversations, he will be fully aware of the conversation he was engaged in. A woman could not only recall her own conversation but the conversations of everyone in the room. We think differently and function differently. In not-so-good relationships, the strengths and weaknesses are problems to one another. They should be complements. We were made to be together and use those strengths and weaknesses as partnerships to produce good results. It can only happen if we understand our differences and put ourselves in the opposite gender's shoes to understand, feel and think as they do.

Sometimes we are offensive to our women because of our insensitivity to our surroundings. They may be upset for days at something they think is an obvious issue. Being men and having that monocular focus when the incident happened, we may have no clue why she is upset. You have to tell a man what is wrong. He wants to know so he can solve the problem. By nature, we are designed to fix the problems but are handcuffed when women assume or think we should know because they do. They are built with that 360 degrees radar. We have binoculars that see straight. We have to learn to process more or be aware that there may be some information that we are missing. Women must understand that the man is indeed ignorant to the problems that may have them upset. Kill them with communication. Talk more and get all of the input out on the table. Solve problems and work together through understanding your differences.

"Do unto others as you would have them do unto you". That's the Golden Rule. You have probably have heard this for as far back as you can remember. Here's my new Golden Rule: "Do unto others as THEY would have you do unto THEM". People may not want to be treated the way you want to be treated.

It was brought to my attention in Gary Chapman's "The 5 Love Languages" that everyone has one of five different Love Languages and we respond best if others speak to us in our language. If you are speaking French and I am speaking Spanish, how will you understand what I am saying? In order for you to understand me and if I really want you to, I have to learn French. I have discovered my true Love Language. It is the one thing that has driven me since I was a child. It is what makes me tick. My Love Language is what motivates me and pushes me forward to do more. My language is "Words of Affirmation". Since this is my language, this is what I speak to others.

For years I have complimented, praised and thanked my wife, Lauren. I would get upset if she didn't jump up and down with excitement from those words. That's what I would have done.

I was speaking my language to her, not hers. I was doing unto her as I would have her do unto me. I'm about 99% sure that her love language is "Acts of Service". I am learning that language so that I can effectively communicate with her. Your most dominant language is what gives you the most pleasure. You or your significant other's Love Language may be "Quality Time", "Receiving Gifts", "Acts of Service" or "Physical Touch". We may speak a little of all five languages, but one is definitely your native tongue. Speaking someone's Love Language is not limited to romantic love. If you are having problems with your teenage daughter, if you want to improve your relationships with co-workers, or if you just need others to be more responsive to you, find out their Love Language and start speaking it.

When people don't respond to the language we are speaking, we tend to speak louder and that makes things worse. Or we stop speaking altogether. How about learning a new language! If "Receiving Gifts" is not her love language, bringing home a rose won't do. If "Physical Touch" isn't what makes him tick, hugs may rub him the wrong way. "Quality Time" may be her love language so you might just have to take walks in the park. Tell her how beautiful she looks and what a wonder person she is, if "Words of Affirmation" make her smile. Cook his dinner or wash his clothes. Run his bath water from time to time if "Acts of Service" is the love language of his heart. He may just cut the grass or paint the house without you asking him to.

CHAPTER 10

Parenting

"Parenting is so much deeper than rules and regulations. A biblical view teaches that parenting is all about the exposure and change of a child's heart."

-Paul David Tripp

We must honor our parents as God commands us to. The respect that children show for parents and adults is lacking today. I think that most can agree with that statement. Why, is the question. Sure, there are a lot of media influences and global shifts in the world on attitude, religion and culture. Things are not like they were yesterday. It's not all the fault of the child. This is something we must look at. No longer can we just say that a child is bad. We can't expect that they are to automatically do right.

In my experience, children are prone to make the bad decision over the good. It is much easier to follow the path of the slight error in judgment. We are built that way. Your children will not honor you just because you are their parent. You did not honor your parents just because they are your parents. It may seem that way, but they built that into you. We must teach our children to honor us. We must teach this generation to honor its elders and the adults they come into contact with every day. Of course they are disrespectful to "grown-ups". No one has taught them to be respectful. Teaching is not giving someone a set of instructions once and expecting them to retain that information forever. We must be constantly teaching and reinforcing principles and correct thinking. Honoring your parents is a two-way street. Give them a reason to honor you. Respect them just as much as you would have them respect you. I have to teach my sons to honor their mother and me, so that one-day in our time of need, they will be there. We must become like Myron, Sr. He taught his children to honor him by doing the things that one would be honored for doing.

Have you developed the love, honor and respect in your children to the point where they will take care of you in a great time of need, or would they toss you in a home, visit you on holidays and put you in the care of others? We must teach them to love us and honor us. The same goes for every other issue this generation has. We have to teach them. If a child doesn't know how to swim, we teach them. If they don't know how to tie their shoes or ride a bike, we teach them. If they don't know how to read, we teach them. We keep teaching until they get it right. If the don't know how to behave, why don't we teach them? If they are not honoring us the way God commands, why are we not teaching? Why are we not teaching this generation to be respectful? We assume that they should automatically do all of these things. They are not going to until we start teaching them to.

Parenting isn't about "do it because I said so", or it's a good idea, or be obedient so that I look like a good parent in front of my peers. It's about applying the gospel in our lives with our children.

Many people think that some are born with good kids. Sin is in each and every one of us. We need to teach our kids to obey their mother the first time. There are techniques and ways of getting the best out of your kids that may be foreign to you. We often do things because our mother did it this way and her mother and so on. That doesn't make it right! If we want different results, we have to do different things.

Men, if the children don't listen to their mother, it's not her fault. It is your fault. You have to model. You can't tell them to respect and listen to their mother unless you do the same, and with all women. We as men must show how precious women are. It starts with us setting an example.

My friend, he's a great father. He was thrown into single parenthood a short time ago and to a young teenage daughter at that. Imagine the strength and courage it takes to pull off such a task in today's society. I'm sure you are thinking about all of the issues a single father would have raising his teenage daughter. I assure you that he is doing a great job. Things are not always smooth as you could imagine, but he loves her dearly. He disciplines firmly and keeps the leash short. His punishments are fair and I would almost always agree that they fit the crime.

The punishment and discipline actions are not leading to much change. He takes away certain privileges that she really values but she continues to make the same infraction time and time again. As a parent, I know it is hard for you to grasp why your child keeps doing the same wrong things over and over even when you strip them of the things they value the most. As kids we are constantly doing wrong. Wrong is built inside of us. It's actually a lot harder to do what's right. It takes effort to be good. Again, in my experience, there are a smaller percentage of children and teenagers who do right naturally. You may have one like that. You should thank God. Maybe it's because of the way you treat that child. Now we must take a step past teaching them right. Do you praise your child? Are you constantly edifying them to others or in front of their friends? Our biggest misconception is that we shouldn't praise them for the things that they should always be doing. We reward our children for big accomplishments. We need to reward them and praise them more for small things that may be big in their eyes. I'm not saying don't discipline or punish for the negative things they do; we do a lot of that. We just need to reward and uplift more. They will do right more often when they know that you are proud of them, and you are constantly verbalizing your feeling of them being a terrific kid.

There is no motivation for doing those everyday chores or making the right decisions when they are not recognized. A simple "great job on taking out the trash without me asking" goes a long way. To a lot of kids, praise is like gold and we don't give it enough. Think about your situations. Are there more negative consequences than positive rewards? I'm not saying that you have to break the bank to get kids to do right, but you do catch more flies with honey. That honey may be staying up an hour later, driving the car to school, cooking their favorite foods, or spending the night at a friend's house. There is no sweeter honey than the sound of your voice praising your child. Tell them constantly how proud you are of the little things they do. Be genuine in your praise and watch how much they do for you. Watch how they transform into the child who genuinely wants to do right.

I was about seven and my neighbor and friend Greg was a couple of years older than me. Out of all of the butt whippings I received as a child, this was to be an epic one. It is the one I will never forget and it was the one that had the most impact and influence on me. I got plenty before that and plenty after that for various reasons because like most little boys I had a head made of stone.

It was Christmas and I received a shiny new bike. Greg got a toolbox loaded with wrenches, sockets and pliers. We decided to take every nut and bolt off of that bike and dismantle it. We did and had every intention of putting that bike back together but the sun started to set and dear ol' Greg had to get home. His tools had to leave as well.

I completely understand my mother's frustration. A new bike, in a hundred pieces! That belt on my bottom was grand! It effectively stopped me from taking apart anything else. The pain and the hurt of that leather eventually went away but something else went away as well. My curiosity of how things work and even more, my willingness to investigate them by breaking them apart and putting them back together was halted. My mother was protecting her investments in those material things that she had worked hard for. Who was I to be ungrateful by destroying them? Prior to that I had destroyed a lot of toys; but this was different. Engineers break things apart, dissect, investigate them, and put them back together even better. It pains me to see my three boys taking apart the toys their mother and I give them. I often want to grab that leather of mine when I see my five-year-old taking a screwdriver to every screw he can find and detaching every wire on his motorized cars and toys, but I don't. They are always taking parts from one object and "attaching" it to another. They never work again as they are intended, but they are learning and growing. They are being creative, breaking things down and building up new.

They may not end up as architects, engineers, or have careers in industrial technology, but I can't take the chance on killing that spirit. We do that with our young people. There's the little girl in class that just won't stop talking and arguing her point. Maybe you break her spirit by constantly forcing her to subdue that passion to be heard and she never becomes the lawyer she was meant to be. Maybe you have a son who rhymes and raps all the time, but you think it is stupid. Maybe he becomes the next Jay-Z or a great spoken word poet if you encourage him or at least don't discourage him. We have to see all of the hidden talents and potential that they have inside of them and help cultivate those gifts. Would there be any comedians if we had no class clowns? There wouldn't be if we always killed their joke.

My father didn't teach me how to love my mother. He didn't teach me a whole lot as I grew up in this world trying to be a man. Right and wrong were concepts that I determined through skewed eyes. Did he bring me to church and teach me about God and how to be a father? No. He taught me that you may do whatever people allow you to do. No matter how it made them feel. Not a single financial principle was passed down to me. Maybe they weren't passed down to him. The cycle must be broken. Fathers who abuse their wives, will have sons who will do the same. Remember the PSA back in the early 90's. "I learned it from watching you!" I am not and do not claim to be perfect or better than you, but there are some things that I have to do differently in my life. There are things that I have to change because they are watching. They will do as I do, not as I say. Are you modeling for your children? Yes you are. The question is, are you doing it in a positive way or a negative one?

Today I think of the value we put on our families and the influence those close family members have on our life and the fulfillment of the purpose God put in our life. I have been blessed to have a loving, nurturing and caring family. There are people who add to you, multiply you, and those who subtract you. Unfortunately, sometimes those who subtract you, are family. Even then, we must identify the sub-tractors and subtract them from our lives. We must protect our spirit from those who willingly or un-knowingly hindering our progress in life. Father "T" would always tell me that the road to hell is paved with good intentions. Mama, daddy, cousin or even Great Aunt Sue may be hurting you because the information they share may not be correct. Because mama did it, grandma did it, and great grandma did it that way, doesn't make it right. Seek knowledge and be careful of the influences of others on your life.

The core unit of society is the family and it is in our homes that these principles must take root and flourish. There is nothing more powerful in history than being a great mother or father. My thought is that the most important thing we can do is to truly succeed in the home. It is a process and often tough. The only way to value family is through family values. If you want to pass on the right traditions, start to develop your family values based on truth. It's not always easy. It's not always fun. You're not always going to want to do it, but it's always going to be worth it.

We blame the youth of today for their ways of life, being lazy, disrespectful, lack of drive and so on. It is not the youth of today, it's the generation that raised them and influenced them or allowed them to be influenced by the negative versus the positive. We need to teach our children to run against the crowd when the crowd is wrong. If we all do that, we can restore the belief in generations to come.

We should be constantly looking to intentionally improve in all areas of our lives. Books provide a lot of the knowledge that can help everyone grow. Those books only contain the needed information. Your wisdom comes from applying that knowledge. Taking action is where you grow, not just knowing. But it is half of the battle. Recently I found a great book in a seemingly unlikely place. It was a roadside gas station that my wife and I stopped at during a mini vacation. It really is a simple yet powerful book. "52 Things Kids Need from A Dad" by Jay Payleitner. As I read through those 52 things, I am blown away by what I'm doing and not doing; the effect I'm having on my boys by being there for them and shaping their lives. As I read the importance of a dad and the things that really need to be done by them for their kids, I get saddened. The reason I get sad is because I know I am not perfect and I fall short; but there are so many young kids that are not getting very much from their dads. The statistics and effects of fatherless children are overwhelming. Even those who just pay child support and occasionally visit them are falling very short from what kids need from their dads. The number one thing you can do is help them beat the odds. The table is stacked against them. Being in their life is the first step to leveling the playing field so that they will have a chance.

CHAPTER 11

Leading Following Mentoring

"Leadership is not about titles or positions. It's about one life influencing another"

-John C. Maxwell

Every one of us is called to lead. At some point in our lives there will be a demand for us to step up to the plate and perform a task that we may not want to engage in, but it will be imperative for us to do so. In that very moment, what will you do? Will you be ready? Are you prepared to lead at this very moment? Your number will be called. The best thing for you and others, who will ultimately depend on your leadership, is to prepare yourself now. We just don't know when that time will come or in what capacity you will be called.

What exactly is leadership? We have to think about this constantly and intentionally focus on it through study. It can be defined as the positive influence to get people moving in the right direction. The right direction may be based on your perspective, moral compass or the mission of a particular unit.

Many people have influence but may not be intentional in their leading, or may not be leading in the right direction. That is not leadership. Throughout my life I have had influence on some that has not always been a positive one. True leadership is something that you can grow into. Sure, many are blessed by being born with natural leadership abilities, but you don't have to discount yourself from the leadership group. We are in desperate need for more leaders around the country. But leadership is not necessarily influencing large groups. It may just be in your home, family or community. You just may need to be a great leader of one, yourself.

Leadership can be developed. Start developing those foundational qualities of a leader. Become hungry and develop your motivation. Your motivation may be success, recognition & respect, and leaving a legacy. Create a vision of where you want to be that is above your current reality. That develops your hunger. Be teachable by yourself and others. You must start your Self-directed Shift with a self-directed education. Eliminate those pitfalls that stop you from growing, like thinking you know everything, not staying focused on your vision, giving in to your bad habits, and not lining up your priorities. Becoming a leader, each person must find their pitfalls and avoid them. The make or break quality of a leader is being honorable. How is your character and integrity? I once read a quote that stated "The Character of a Man is the only thing that will walk back from the grave into the hearts of the people who knew him." Have the character to do what you say you're going to do and be where you say you're going to be. Live by your word. Today this is lacking more than ever. No one will follow you if you can't be trusted. No one will allow you to lead if they don't believe that you will deliver what you say you will deliver. Leadership can be developed. "If you call yourself a leader and no one is following, then you're just out for a walk."

When I got home the other day, my five-year-old kindergarten son was very excited to tell me that he was the line leader in his class for the day. His face was like a neon sign. He was lit up with excitement just to tell me the news. Imagine how he felt being the line leader. I remember those days. Everyone wanted to be the leader. Everyone couldn't wait for their turn, their turn to walk proudly at the front of the line as their peers followed.

With my personality, I had to make my turn unique and special. I zigged and zagged. Sometimes I would hop, wave my arms or slap hands with oncoming classes like at the end of a little league baseball game. The twenty or so kids behind me did everything I did. They followed my every step. Sometimes it was hard to come up with clever things to do that didn't cross the line and get me into trouble. I led my way and everyone else led in his or her own way. There was no right or wrong way to lead and everyone wanted to do it. When did we stop wanting to lead and just wanted to follow? In my opinion, it's when we figured out that leading takes work. It became more than just doing something cool and making those behind you mimic your actions. At some point the reality of leading will become clear. To lead you must serve those who are following you. You must do what benefits them the most. If what you are doing is not right, everyone will suffer or those behind you will stop and turn to another direction. It becomes easier to just follow because you can just put your faith in the leader and move in their direction. Not everyone is what we would call leaders, but everyone will be called to lead at some point. Are you ready to lead? Do you want to lead? Can you lead? Others will need you.

My wife is a great leader and mother to our children because she serves our kids every day. She does what's best for them every minute of every day. She has led our family for years when I simply just followed. I thank her for her courage, strength and leadership as a wife and mother. At some point, I decided to get out of line and move to the front. I was called to lead and take my position at the front. Our families, churches, schools, country and communities are running short of people ready to take their place as line leader. To the school kids, you are not too young to lead. To the older generation, it's not too late. You can start leading now. To those in-between, what are you waiting for? The world is calling you to lead. Step up and take charge. Do the right things and others will follow you where you need them to go.

Most people are walking in lines or packs doing what the person in front of them is doing. They are following the rules and conforming to whatever system society has determined to be normal. It may be financial and economic trends, marital standards, educational avenues or political stands. Every so often, someone gets out of line and says, "Not me. You guys are going the wrong way." Those people do the unpopular thing and go the other direction. Because everyone is doing it, doesn't make it right. Just because your mother is in that line just ahead of you and grandma went that way years ago, doesn't mean you have to follow. Be that leader that stands up and organizes others to move in the right direction. Everyone will not follow you. You only need to inspire a few that understand, that the new direction you are heading is a path much more worth traveling. Those people will inspire others and those will inspire more and more until the direction of a family, a community, and other groups of likeminded people are getting better results in life.

Whether you know it or not, people are waiting for someone to lead. They are waiting on you. We need an excuse to get out of that line. We know we don't belong in it, but it is hard to just jump out. Someone is in front of us and someone is behind. There is a leader in each one of us.

Sometimes we must follow the right people first before we can lead. I watched people jump out of that line and head the other way. No one pulled me out. That would have made me jump back in. No one can force us to change. We have to want to connect to the right things by following people with the right results. I tell stories of my growth and change to open ears with the hope that others can relate. Then maybe the shift starts to take shape in those around me, and change begins in the lives of the people close to me who need it and want it. You don't need permission to lead people. They are waiting on you to step up. Most people are not going to ask you to lead them out of the darkness even though they don't want to be there. Challenge the status quo, create a community of people leading people and creating other leaders. Start something positive today that others will join in. Start some kind of movement and stick to it. It won't take much. It will be like a snowball moving downhill. We just need more people starting something good.

A professional athlete should not be your role model. They shouldn't be your children's role models. It is okay for them to be an inspiration for attaining big dreams. But a role model, I don't think so. In my early professional baseball career, I participated in quite a few baseball camps for young kids. One particular little boy who came to our camps and was at every home game told me that he wanted to be just like me. His mother told me once that he really looked up to me. I was his role model. The crazy thing is that this little boy or his mother knew nothing of my character. All they knew of me is how hard I threw a baseball and the passion I had on the field. They didn't know the troubling issues I had outside of my profession.

My personal life was not one that you would want to expose to others looking up to you as a role model. My choices and decision-making back then was not something I am proud of. Look at all these celebrities and professional athletes in the news for personal misconduct. Spousal abuse, drugs and a multitude of arrests headline the news and social networks about our beloved television personalities. Our children look up to them as role models. When they act certain ways and do certain things that are contrary to our moral values, our children follow. If their favorite athlete does it, they think that it's okay. There are some good professional athletes and celebrities out there, but we don't know them that well. They are not in our lives on personal levels.

There are some role models that we do have personal relationships with. Young people, you have parents, teachers, pastors, policemen and local business owners to look up to. They are accomplishing great things in this tough world. Parents, teachers, pastors, policemen and everyone in the community, they are watching you. Children need better role models. They need us to do the right things. They need us to give them someone to look up to. Are your actions worthy of being copied by your children and your neighbor's children? Good or bad those actions will be duplicated. They need to look up to you. There is no better role model than a good mother or father. Parents make the best role models.

There is a call for leadership in this world. We need more leaders in our country, the government, our community, our schools and most of all our families. We must lead our homes. What does it mean to lead? To lead is to serve. Are we truly serving others in our lives? Or are we putting ourselves first and then tending to the needs of those entrusted to our care?

Often I see people in positions of leadership who are not leading. You may be in that position but no one is following.

There are times in my life when I look back and see no one. Why is that? It is because you have to truly serve others. You have to do things that make you worthy of being followed and you have to do those things consistently over time. Those closest to you, those who have known you the longest, will often be some of the last to follow you. Why is it that way? It is because they knew you at times in your life when you didn't make the best decisions. They knew you when you committed acts unworthy of being followed.

There are so many things that have happened in our past that we try to forget and wish others did too, but those close to us keep those things ingrained in their memory to remind them of who they believe you are. When I was sixteen years old, I would drive my 1975 Sedan Deville from the passenger side. It was crazy and people got a kick out of it. There were so many things that I did that were completely out of character. How can anyone listen to me talk on peace and conflict resolution when I was the first to strike a blow in a fight? Maybe you've been to jail, betrayed a loved one, were the neighborhood drunk, or maybe at one-point God held no significance in your life. Just keep leading.

Continue to do the right things. Commit acts that make you worthy of being followed consistently over time. Continue to serve. It is very easy for those who don't know your past to follow your lead. They can only judge you by who you are, not who you were. They can only see the person and the qualities that you now possess. All we can do and all we need to do, is take on a life of serving others and those in doubt will eventually follow.

So, I have been sick. You have watched me battle this disease for years. You've witnessed the toll that it has put on my family. Recently I have found the cure! The medicine! It was given to me from a person who had suffered the same ailment. I have not fully recovered but I am in the treatment process and getting better everyday. You compliment me on how well I'm getting. You see the change and you are happy for me. The problem is that you suffer the same disease. You have known it all along but were afraid to expose your condition. What we fail to realize is that conditions get worse when left untreated. I see the progression of the disease in you. You complain about your situation. You are looking for help and don't know where to get it. I offer you my pills because I know the pain you are experiencing and truly want what is best for you.

Weeks go by and you stare at the medication on your dresser or counter top. Not one pill has made its way into your body and the rapid progression of the disease is obvious to everyone around you. I use this analogy often when talking to people about fixing problems in their life. Why is it that people are offered help and then refuse to accept the solution that has worked for others? I know that all medicine does not do the same thing or have the same effect on everyone, but at some point you have to take a chance on something that has worked in the lives of others. Standing in the batter's box when I played baseball, I knew if I didn't swing, I would not hit a homerun. I figured that I at least had a chance if I would take the bat off my shoulder and swing.

We can't take advice from everyone. Uncle Ray is dead broke and has been his whole life. Don't listen to Ray when he tells you to how to get your finances in order. Don't listen to Samantha on how to hold your marriage together. I know she's your best friend, but she's been married a few times and her relationships never seem to be on the right path. You have to find those with fruit on the tree. Find people with value in their information. We must follow people who are leading in the directions we need to go.

The answers we all are looking for are out there. There is no problem that has not been gone through by someone else. There are books in this world that are worth their weight in diamonds!

Listen to people who you trust and admire. Take time to study the ways of others who have traveled the roads before you and are on the path clearing the trails. When you follow leaders you can develop your own leadership skills. Experience is not the best teacher. Someone else's experience should be better because it's an opportunity to learn without the consequence of pain associated with trial and error. Sir Isaac Newton once wrote, " If I have seen further, it is because I have stood on the shoulders of giants."

The other morning I was blessed with the privilege of meeting with and being mentored by a giant. With his 6'9" frame he is truly a giant of a man; but his character, integrity and inner body is much bigger. He is constantly working to improve himself and he is still growing. Up early in the morning before the sun could even peek its head above the horizon, I found myself driving to visit him to seek counsel and guidance in my own personal development and growth. I feel privileged to have him as my mentor and I am excited to have other strong mentors to listen to and point me in the right direction. We all should be mentoring others and be willing to be mentored. Mentors look out for the best interest of others by their experiences and knowledge from walking the walk.

Our greatest and most precious resource is our time. What an honor it is to have someone give of their time and lend their shoulders for you to see a bit further down the road. How could I waste his time by not utilizing the information shared with me to the benefit of my growth? Are you being mentored? Are you mentoring others? Look for someone. Seek help and guidance from those qualified to give it. Seek others looking to eat from your fruit. We all have something to offer to others who have less than ourselves. Be intentional in your growth and in the growth of those around you. Mentoring is the key.

Imagine Michael Jordan without Phil Jackson; LeBron James and D. Wade with no Erik Spoelstra back when they won championships together; or Tom Brady and no sight of Bill Belichick. For those of you who are confused at this point, they're all star athletes with their coaches. The best people in the world need coaches. Michael Jordan couldn't have won six NBA championships with no coach sitting on the side directing his actions, watching his back, and giving insight to the whole picture. Life is a game and we are on that court or football field playing the best we can without a coach, without someone looking out for our best interests. Can we play without a coach? Yes. Will the time run out? Yes. What will the scoreboard read? How much better would it be if you played this game with Phil Jackson on your bench? You see, we get very emotional, we get excited, and we get overwhelmed by all of the players in the game, all of the plays, the fouls and the penalties. Sometimes we have to sit out for a while to get ourselves together. We believe, because we are good, we don't need help. We act as if we are doing just fine when the scoreboard says otherwise.

Coaches can see things that you can't see. They are watching your blind spots. When I was a High School pitcher, I had very little success until my coach started calling the pitches that I was throwing. He was watching everything and knew what would work and what wouldn't. Sometimes being on the outside looking in is a great thing. Coaches have a different perspective. Imagine being in a boxing ring fighting for your life and there's no one in your corner telling you to keep your hands up, move your feet, or throw the jab. Sure, you could win, but the odds are better with some direction from someone on the outside of those ropes. How well would you do with a personal trainer every time you went to the gym or a nutritionist to help you with your dieting? We need coaches in our lives. We need life coaches. We need people with fruit on the tree, helping us achieve the goals we are fighting for. Why would you not have a coach who helps you develop your relationships with others?

The problems that you are going through and the situations that are troubling you have been dealt with already. Your situation is nothing new. It's just new to you. Why not seek counsel from those who have mastered certain steps in this game? Just be careful of your choice in coaches. Just about everyone would be willing to be your coach, but not everyone is qualified. You can, but you don't have to play this game without a coach. Find a mentor. Find someone you can trust and that has fruit growing on their limbs. Find someone willing to help cultivate and harvest the fruit that you are capable of producing. Let your pride go. If you need help, seek it. Whether you admit it or not, whether you want it or not, we all could use help. We all can improve. We all can do better at this game. We all can win. Put me in coach. I'm ready to play! I'm ready to win.

He was eager to learn and wanted as much knowledge as I could give. He went to many photographers and professionals in the business only to be turned away. Like a lost puppy looking for food, he was hungry and not one of those people would share their food. That was years ago when I was in the middle of pursuing my own professional photography business and teaching high school photography classes. He couldn't understand why others were not willing to give of their talents and wisdom. Most people in business and trades hoard information from others seeking to excel in the same areas. They fear competition and worry that others will surpass them in success. I have always been one to give of what I have learned to those seeking the same information.

There are a half dozen former students of mine who have become part of my competition. They are getting clients who could possibly be my clients. That actually makes me proud to have had a hand in their success. The self-directed shift starts with a self-directed education. I gave the young man as much information as I thought he needed to begin his success track. I gave of my books, my knowledge, technical advice and even my self-developed "tricks of the trade" in printing.

Today he is one of the most impressive illustrations of the Self-directed shift. He works harder and more efficiently than any photographer in the business. He took it upon himself to delve into a self-directed education because he was looking for a shift in his knowledge and abilities to produce as a master photographer. He is on his way by reading books, applying the principles and developing his craft. He is so focused on becoming the best he can be that nothing will stop him.

Talking shop with him is an amazing experience every time we sit down. The student has become the teacher. In photography, he has surpassed what I could have taught him, and I couldn't be more proud of that fact. His career has taken off because he decided to create a shift by learning as much about photography as he could on his own. He couldn't wait for someone to give him the formula or the keys to his own success. Teddy had to go get it himself. You will have to do the same in the areas of your life that you want to create a shift. He looked for mentors and many weren't willing to help. So, he found some of his best mentors in books, audios and YouTube clips. He read magazine after magazine on the subject. Sometimes in some areas whom you follow and what you follow may not be a person or thing you can physically touch. You can have a mentor that you've never met. You may not personally know me but are being mentored through my words in this book.

We're all learning and growing as human beings. Do you share your knowledge and promote the growth of others around you? Do you hold back on giving good information to people seeking that knowledge because you are afraid of them becoming more successful or making you look smaller? Does competition bother you? It shouldn't. It should push you to find your niche and force you into better creative positions. Give of your knowledge. Share your wisdom. Help others achieve what you have achieved. Help eliminate the struggle in their life because you can show them the way. That is being a leader. We must decide what matters in life before we can live a life that matters.

CHAPTER 12

Fear, Failure & Excuses

"Before success comes in any man's life, he's sure to meet with much temporary defeat and, perhaps some failures. When defeat overtakes a man, the easiest and the most logical thing to do is to quit. That's exactly what the majority of men do."

-Napoleon Hill

Fear, failure and excuses are robbing us of our true treasures. They are not allowing us to get on the path of success. Fear is said to be false evidence appearing real. There are so many people who are afraid of things that have almost no chance of happening. Some are even fearful of success because they haven't experienced very much of it and don't know what they would do if they have it. Many people turn and run when they fail, but is not hitting the mark really failure? Coming up short or just shy of our goals is part of human nature. Excuses are our way of rationalizing why we are not doing what we can be doing, achieving, or living the live we want to live.

Facing your fears is much easier than avoiding them. The more you avoid your tough situation, the more the fear builds. I was about seven years old when our whole family went to an amusement park on Lake Pontchartrain in Louisiana. I was so afraid of the roller coaster and it didn't even twist and loop. All of my male cousins, family and friends were trying to get me on that ride. They all got on, but I didn't. I remember crying because they were trying to force me to get on. "You'll see. It will be okay. It's no big deal. You will like it when you get on." No amount of words could convince me that it would be okay.

Fast forward to one summer, twenty plus years later. We were at Six Flags in Dallas and Lathan, my middle son wanted to ride everything. He was so brave. I was not! There was one particular ride that I was extremely terrified to get on, but he wanted to ride it. We held hands as we walked through the long line all the way to the top. I can't recall facing any greater fear as a man. I had to show him that I was strong and that it was just a ride. By the time we got in the cart I wanted to scream, get off and turn around. I was shaking so badly and he was just as calm and ready. I have avoided these rides my whole life and the fear had built to an excruciating pain. The cart took off and the adrenaline kicked in. It was awesome.

Most of the fear had left because I had done "the thing". The ride was over but some fear was still there. Lathan wanted to ride it again and ride even more thrilling rides, so we did. The more we did, the more the fear dissipated. Whatever fears you are facing in life, take them head on. The fear of the thing is usually bigger than the thing. The fear grows the more you avoid the thing. I can't say it enough. Do the thing you fear and the death of fear is certain. Once you start doing the things you fear, you will start doing more because you will realize that you were making much more of them than necessary.

There will be a domino effect in your behavior. You will look to conquer the things that you fear. Thanks to my son for forcing me to face the fear that I had no reason to fear. The fear of the thing is bigger than the thing. Do the thing and kill the fear.

We all have dreams and goals in life. If you don't, you are doing yourself a big injustice. Get a dream! Every kid has those huge ambitions. What happens? Why do so many people fail or quit going after the things that are worthy? Someone just like you had that same dream and accomplished it. What causes the failures and what causes some to give up?

Often attaining great things makes you look foolish to others because you are not doing what the crowd is doing. Your pride kills you because we are so worried about what others think or say. Some people are "ate-up" with some type of internal condition that they will not address and fix. It may be an addiction or underlying flaw that no one knows about because they hide their problems well from the world. There was a thing or two that I had to conquer. There are things, problems and issues in each one of our lives that we must conquer. We are distracted so easily. We lose focus and soon our car has drifted off the road or into oncoming traffic. Crash! Maybe your issue is settling for comfort. You were heading for something great but you stopped at good. Maybe you wanted to be a doctor and you settled for being a nurse, or you became a teacher whose ambition stopped, but you wanted to be a principal. The dream may not be big enough. A big dream evokes passion and passion evokes the drive to win. You need a big dream and a lot of passion. That dream doesn't have to be big to me. It has to be big to you. It has to get you off of the couch and moving.

Another area is personal responsibility. How much of your failure is your fault? All of it! If you take 100% of the blame, you can take control of correcting it. It's all up to you. For some people, self-doubt slowly creeps up; and then like a ton a bricks it hits. The belief is gone. "It just wasn't meant to be" or "I knew I couldn't do it". If you let that doubt creep in, it will slowly take over and cripple you. This last reason I would like to share is one that is so heavily ingrained in this new emerging generation. It is the lack of mental toughness. It's not just in that generation. It's in us all these days. We baby ourselves and we baby our kids. We want things to be easier for us and easier for those coming after us. At some point we must develop the minds to withstand the battery of artillery that will try to stop us from succeeding at life and achieving all the good and worthy things we want. Take your dream. If you've lost it, get it back. Steer clear of those reasons why we fail or quit, and fight to bring that dream into your possession.

There was always a reason that I didn't get certain results in my life that had nothing to do with me. There was always some type of entity to blame that was out of my control. Every now and then I would take the blame but only to a certain degree. I eventually started taking partial blame for my misfortunes. There was always a "but" at the end of statements where I took any blame. Most of the time those statements started off with "If". If this would have happened, if she would have, or if I had more of this or that, were always the answers to why I didn't succeed or didn't get the desired results I was looking for. I always wanted many things in life and there were always reasons I didn't get them. I never had control of those reasons. Until now! If something happens to hinder my progress in what I am striving for or trying to attain, I take 100% of the blame or responsibility. There is no reason to shift the responsibility to anything or anyone else for me not achieving. You can do this. It may not be your fault, but it is your responsibility when it comes to your own success. This is a new attitude or philosophy. It doesn't mean that you really caused certain things to happen or not in your life. It is just a concept of taking responsibility.

When you take 100% of the responsibility for the results in your life, it means you have the power to correct wrongs and steer your ship into the right direction when it is off course. Putting the blame elsewhere means that you can't change anything. Shifting the blame means that you have no control of outcomes. You do have control. Everything you receive in your life is in your own power. We control much more than we believe in life. Your destiny is in your own hands. Stop putting faults in your life on others. So what if your mother was a drug addict! You're not. Don't put the blame of your life on her. Take responsibility. Maybe you are on drugs right now. It's not the dealer's fault for selling the stuff to you or your cousin's fault for giving you that first hit. Take 100% responsibility for making your life the life you've always wanted. Stop the blame game. We look for excuses to why our lives suck. Usually we say it is someone else's fault. No, it's not! Your job, your bank account, your relationships, your education, and everything in your life is your responsibility.

You may need to cure yourself from the illness of excuses. An excuse is a failure disease. In my opinion, it puts more people on bed rest and in early graves than anything the CDC has on its list. Excuses are even communicable. They spread like a plague. I made hundreds of excuses why I didn't do this or that. We find ourselves making them over and over in our lives. It is endless the amount of excuses people make who fail at their goals or dreams. Most people have some form of this disease. Study the lives of people with success. They have the same obstacles and roadblocks as everyone else. Often they have greater struggles because they fight through the small ones and get to even bigger ones. They just don't make excuses! That is the difference.

Once a person with the failure disease has found a "good' excuse, he sticks with it. Then he relies on it to explain to himself and others why he is not moving forward. Every time the excuse is made, it is driven deeper into the sub-conscious. The disease gets worse.

Yesterday I visited a teacher's room and noticed a poster on her wall that read "Aim for the moon and if you don't succeed at least you will be among stars". I was reminded of it last night as I watched my wife gaze out of the window looking for the meteor shower that was supposed to take place. The point of that poster is to aim high and if you don't succeed or if you fail, you will still reach great things. Why would anyone teach falling short or failure? It's because failure is a part of our human nature. What does failure mean to you? What is your attitude about falling short of your goals and dreams? So many people are afraid of failure that they never fail. They never do anything risky or worthwhile that is not guaranteed through consistently working towards those goals. Whether you realize it or not, we fail every day. It is truly a part of being human. What I've observed in life is that many of us miss our targets in life an overwhelming majority of the time. We miss the mark in relationships, financial goals, education, and in so many more areas. The point was never made more clear to me than when my pitching coach in the minor leagues told me that we all fail all the time, but we can use that to our advantage.

I was struggling throwing strikes in one bullpen session so he asked me what was I focusing on. I told him that I was focusing on the catcher and where he was setting up on the plate. Because we fail, I was throwing all around him. He then told me to focus on the catcher's mitt. I started missing all around the mitt. That was a good thing. I was getting excited. Then he told me to focus on one small part in the inside of the mitt. I started hitting the mitt every time.

We can harness the power of our failures by focusing on specific detailed things. We may fail, but get so close to the specific goal that it won't even matter that we didn't hit the bull's eye right dead in the center. We still win. Just being on the path to the target is success because you are actively engaged in growth and movement that millions don't even attempt. Too often our focus is general and our goals become wishful thinking. We need to narrow our focus to specific attainable things and fight with all our might to reach them. Author Jack Canfield once set a goal to make $100,000. Do you think he was upset when he only made $92,000? No. Getting that close prompted him to set new goals. Aim high but aim specific. You don't have to fail but if you do, you will land in a comfortable position ready to aim again. We should get fired up when we get close but come up a little short. We can learn so much by that experience that can help us in the next try. You can fail your way closer and closer every time you restart your endeavor.

Let's reframe what failure is. Ninety-five percent of failure is not failure at all. Failure is quitting or giving up. Quitting is another failure disease. And yes, it's just as contagious as excuses. I hate seeing young people who quit at things because I know that that disease will only become greater with time if it's not cured.

Why do people quit doing things that are worthy? Pride kills people. You are unwilling to look like a fool because you didn't hit your mark. There are certain amounts of failure that have to come before you can have success. Abraham Lincoln failed horribly his whole life. Study him. He had lost almost every political position he ran for. He looked like a fool to many because he wouldn't stop trying. If you asked a hundred people to name five presidents, ninety-nine percent would say "Lincoln". Most of us couldn't lose that much and keep going. It is said that Thomas Edison failed at making viable light bulb filament over a thousand times. He got it right the last time and we all benefit from it today. How many times have you quit after one or two tries? Don't worry about what people think. The people that we are worried about are the ones that wouldn't even show up for our funeral. Out of the ones who would show up, most of them would be there only if the weather was good. Why worry about their opinions about what you are doing? If the end result is a worthy cause, get on that path and keep moving. Just keep moving. If you fall, get up and keep moving. You are on a Self-directed Shift. You are creating a great separation of results in areas of your life that the average people are not. Their opinions don't matter. Lose your pride and gain your dream.

So many people talk and talk and talk about their situation. They complain but attempt no actions. They don't know if the actions they would attempt will solve the problem or lead to the completion of the challenge. It doesn't really matter! You just have to do something. If you do nothing, it will end in no result. Doing something, even something not quite right, will give you measurable results. Once you have started a process of trying to solve the issue, you can adjust. You will always have to make adjustments. Overcoming adversity is the mark of great character. If you follow that formula over and over in every challenge of your life you will succeed. Identify the issue and make a plan. Take actions to get the results you want. Measure your progress and then adjust as needed to keep yourself on track. We all have problems we must face in our lives. All are different and some are larger than others. You may face your problem and conquer it, but the fact of life is that another one is coming. You will always have roadblocks in your life but you can't go ahead until you face the one that is in front of you right now. Face the fear. Avoiding the roadblock won't get you to where you are trying to go. Stopping keeps you right in that spot or pushes you backwards at an alarming rate. You can turn around and try to find other ways to go but it will take you forever and there may be more roadblocks on the other streets. The quickest way is straight ahead through the issues, putting them behind you, and reaching your destination.

CHAPTER 13

The Self

"I count him braver who overcomes his desires than him who conquers his enemies; for the hardest victory is over self."

-Aristotle

You have so many talents. Each one of us human beings is born with so much potential for greatness. The infinite amount of power we possess rarely is tapped into by an overwhelming majority of those walking this earth. Imagine if we all reached for the highest levels of that potential. Heaven would truly be on earth. The sky would be the limit to the lives we could live. The problem is that many don't understand that there is that infinite greatness lying inside of them waiting to be unleashed. If they only knew it was there and could bring it out, I believe more people would be succeeding. We have to look at who we are inside and out, compare and contrast between what produces fruit or not, make necessary adjustments in our philosophy, attitude, and actions, and get the results we desire. Our Self-directed Shift has to start with self. You are the key.

Let me start with a series of questions. How many times have you been to the barbershop or the hair salon this year? What about getting your fingernails and toes manicured and pedicured? Have you visited a tanning bed or had your skin professionally exfoliated? Can you calculate the amount of money that you have spent on new clothing and fancy jewelry? How many new pairs of shoes have you purchased this year? How much time has been spent in the mirror making sure that you look good? There is nothing wrong with doing all of those things and more, but let's compare that with the amount of money you've spent on your personal growth and your inward self. What is your ratio of shoes to books? Have you been to a leadership, personal development, or spiritual growth seminar? Have you listened to a self-help audio this year? How much time has been spent on developing your character and improving your integrity?

The majority of people I come across work very hard on their outward appearance and spend much time, effort and money doing so. Again, I say to you that there is nothing wrong with that. The problem is the balance of taking care of the more important side of our whole being. That's our inside. How much spiritual time do you give yourself? I venture to say that most give very little outside of the hour or two on Sundays during church service. How many don't even bother to do that much!

The Self-directed shift starts with you. It's all about you getting off of the path traveled by the masses. I see so many people cheering on their favorite sports teams. It hurts me to see the people I love and care about push for LeBron and Kobe to win, but they don't even push for their own victories. I guess they don't believe that they can truly win. NBA teams and players have already made it. There is no need for me to cheer them on. That's what the crowd is doing. Run against the herd. The Self-directed path is a path of few. It's okay if you're a fanatic, stay glued to the television during the play-offs, or feel like you're in the game with your favorite player, but who is cheering you on in this game of life? Are you rooting for your own victories? Are you doing the things in your life to get to the championship? Some people find it hard to believe that I was once a professional athlete and for over a year in a half I have not even seen an NBA game, an MLB game, or an NFL contest except for the Super Bowl.

I'm working on my own victory. I'm out in the world trying to help others achieve their own victories. There are people I know personally who are looking for a better way. My favorite television shows were "Baseball Tonight" and "Sports Center". I haven't seen either in two years and I don't miss them because they were not adding value to my life. I have hit more goals and have gotten closer to all of the dreams I have for my family in the past couple of years than the previous ten. It's because I could care less which team of millionaires holds up the gold ball at the end of the season. The team that I want to see win is my family and friends that are fighting for our own victories. By no means am I saying that you shouldn't enjoy sports and television. I just believe that you should be fighting for your own victory more than you cheer for those sports stars you admire so much. It would take very little time to transform the poor results in your life into the results you want and deserve. Try reading ten pages of a life-changing book every day. It's a simple task to do; but it's easy not to do so most people don't do it. Listen to self-improvement audios and associate with others of like minds. Watch your life change for the better. Victory is yours if you want it.

Be realistic and evaluate yourself. Are you devoting the same amount of time and energy to your insides as you do to your outsides? Maybe you have heard the saying, "Beauty is only skin deep, but you're ugly to the bone". Growth and success come from the inside. We have to align right thinking, moral values, character and integrity from deep inside our souls with our outward actions, persona and appearance. Our insides influence our outsides. We worry about our outsides because that builds our reputation. Reputation is only what others think of us. It's not who we truly are. Our character is the core of who we really are, and character can only be developed from within. Over time, our character takes over our reputation and gives our outside its shape. The outside can never overshadow or build what is within. Continue to take care of your outside but put just as much effort into who you really are. Work on your insides. Character counts, but there is no way you can just focus on the inside either.

The Self-directed Shift is about creating change in any area as well as all areas and aspects of your life to become a better you with better results.

In a panic I threw on my seatbelt and sat up straight in my old beat-up truck. I usually have my seatbelt on. After school I was driving into what I could see was a roadblock a few hundred feet ahead. The officer asked for my driver's license and proof of insurance. I handed him my license and fumbled through my wallet for the insurance card. After a few seconds, he stopped me and said, " I trust you. Go ahead". I noticed he took a glance at me and quickly surveyed the interior of my car. I was ecstatic that he let me go because I didn't have an insurance card with me. Could it have been my appearance? I was dressed in a pressed button-down shirt and necktie to match. My facial hair was trimmed and neat. Not a word came out of my mouth and there was a small stack of books on my seat. He didn't know me from Adam, but he said that he trusted me.

It reminded me of a chapter in a book I had read on appearance, and I knew it was a lesson I would read and teach to my sons that night. You don't have to say a word. Your appearance often speaks for you. Not only does your appearance speak for you, it breathes feelings into your soul. Those feelings breathe actions. If you look like a million bucks, you will feel and act like a million bucks.

Whether you think it's fair or not, you will be judged by your appearance. It doesn't matter that you are a great person of integrity and outstanding character. Look at yourself and try to think of what a person who does not know you would think of you, if they were setting their eyes on you for the first time. We can't help it sometimes. We are judgmental. Oftentimes I am wrong when judging students by their appearance that takes my classes and I get to know them. Many people won't get to know you because they may not be able to get past the way you are dressed, your crazy hairstyle, or your body piercings. You may be giving potential employers or prospective partners the wrong impressions.

For a short period of my life I wore "dreadlocks". For weeks I visited business after business trying to solicit help for a wonder children's program I had put together. Door after door was slammed in my face without me being able to get more than two words out of my mouth. They didn't want to hear what I had to say. The "nappy" hair was like flashing lights warning of danger. The jeans and t-shirts didn't do much good either. I cut my hair and put on a shirt and tie. The difference was like having red carpet in those doorways that were once slammed in my face. I didn't change who I was. The change was people's impression or perception of me. That was simply done by the way I was dressed. When I am dressed-to-impress, I also think better of myself. When I dress up, I gain more confidence and others sense that confidence. Look important and you will feel important. Feel important and you will act important. Act important and others will think that you are important. They will treat you as if you are important because you are important! Everything starts with your appearance. Pull your pants up, tuck your shirt in, fix your hair, wear clothes that flatter your figure, paint your nails, and wear a smile.

She spends about an hour and a half to get ready for an evening out at the nightclub. Not one strand of hair is out of place. Her lipstick color has changed eight times in the last hour. He goes to the gym 3-4 times a week. He has sculpted his abs by engaging in a twenty-minute nightly routine so that he can walk the beach with no shirt on. Sitting on the beach yesterday, my wife took several pictures of me with her cellphone. I have to say that I was not pleased with any one of them. I even tried to pose myself in a flattering position so that I could at least fool myself. I once had a body that was in decent shape. The fact is that I have not spent a lot of time on my outer appearance. I have been working on my inner self. Do you spend as much time on your inside as you do your outside? What would people see if that could see past the make-up, muscles, the designer dress, the Ralph Lauren Polo Shirt, Louis bag, and 6-inch heels. What if, for one day, we wore our "inside self" on the outside? Would construction workers whistle when you walk by or would they turn their heads? Would your friends think of you as such a tough guy or one of genuine compassion for others? What does your inside look like? What are you spending your time working on? You and your husband look very good standing there holding hands with your matching rings, color-coordinated outfits and occasional hugs. That is what everyone sees. What is the real image of what is inside of you? Are you putting in just as much time developing your character, relationships and integrity as you are putting in time working on your outer appearance? It doesn't take much to strengthen your marriage from within. It doesn't take much to develop yourself as a trustworthy person even if you have had issues in your past. Evaluate yourself today. What do I look like on the inside? What would others think of me if they could see the real me? Be honest with yourself. On a scale of 1-10, where do I rank in my inner beauty, personal skills, integrity, character and self-worth? If it is not 10, then you should be working on yourself. If you say that it is a 10, then you should really be working on yourself. No one is perfect and no one ever will be, but we all should be working to be perfect.

Today we must have posture. We must have a swagger about ourselves to show others that what we believe, we really believe. Others must understand that you have conviction by the way you speak. You don't have to be over the top and push others away. You just have to show pride in your ideals, principles and virtues. We don't need to be over the top in professing our faith or any of our beliefs. We just need to be over the top in our beliefs themselves. Others don't have to believe what we believe. We don't need to change everyone by pushing our agendas down their throats. We just need that posture that says, "I'm proud of who I am. I'm proud of what I do. I'm proud of the choices I make." That swagger is hard not to recognize. It's hard not to want to imitate. Speak up! Talk a little louder, project your voice, hold your chin up, and walk a little faster. Show confidence in yourself. You are the only person who has to believe what you believe. You don't have to make anyone else understand what is inside of you. It will seep out of your pores. Your skin will be saturated with the sweat of your confidence. Produce the posture and develop the swag. You know that feeling you get when you get dressed up really nice? Think about how you feel when you put on that elegant black dress or that suit and tie. Find that feeling in your spring-cleaning clothes, your Saturday morning car-wash attire, or those dingy old sweats. No matter what you wear, develop your posture and find your swagger. When people look into your eyes, they will see what's inside. When they see your walk from a mile away, they will know that you have swagger.

People are watching you. There are many eyes and ears in this world. They are all around us even when they don't make themselves appear. Everything you do is being watched. Everything you say is being heard. Your actions will be duplicated, ridiculed, or dismissed as irrelevant. I've talked about modeling before. Good or bad, your actions will be duplicated. Remember that everything will be seen whether you think so or not.

Have you ever noticed physically handicapped people who do extraordinary things? You can watch the news or look in the papers that show people with no legs running marathons, people with no arms doing the seemingly impossible, the blind man doing the tasks that are hard for the seeing, the extremely poor becoming tremendously wealthy, and others that have some type of huge handicap that they get over. Most of us are perfectly fine. We are the average people blessed with all of our senses, limbs and abilities to do anything. Why does it take someone with less to show us what is possible? They are motivated because they have to prove that their handicaps are not going to stop them from doing the things that everyone else takes for granted. We are born into this world and our environment shapes and molds us. We accept things for what they are or for what they appear to be. We live in a wealthy society. The richest part of this world and at the richest time in history.

The conversation with a friend of mind yesterday was very enlightening. He grew up in an era when there was a struggle and causes to fight for. He grew up in the midst of the fight for civil rights and desegregation. Today we are so comfortable in mediocrity that we don't fight for anything. The fight is what propels us to the top of society. The fight is what gains us the better jobs, relationships and freedoms. We are not fighting. We are accepting life and life is not handing out special gifts to those sitting on the couch. There are many disabled people and people with handicaps that are far from being able to do normal things. Their drive to accomplish normal tasks that we take for granted pushes them far past our normal ability. So imagine what you can do with your perfect body, 20/20 vision, and freedom of living where you are.

When I played baseball, the players from the Dominican Republic were so hungry to succeed. They just wanted what I had, which I didn't think was much. I had a modest American house with food in the refrigerator, television, a car, and a few dollars in my pocket. That motivation to have some of the things that we consider normal has propelled some of those guys to gain a lot more than what I have. The United States has the largest middle class in the world. We are a part of the largest group of people being average and doing average things. You don't have to settle for average because we all have the ability to do well above average. You just need the motivation of those who are without. You need the motivation of people with handicaps that refuse to accept their condition. You need the motivation of those who are not better than you, but choose to do more than you to gain better results than the ones you are currently producing. My hat goes off to all of those people out there who have been limited by physical, mental or any other handicaps but refuse to accept those as limitations. My hat goes off to you for doing more than I in situations where I am truly capable but have not been willing to fight.

Let's just say that I know a few people who have been incarcerated in America's prison system. Why is it that a lot of these guys get out, and for a while at least, are on top of the world? I have recently talked to a couple of people who have done time in state and federal prisons. I was in search of a few answers. Believe it or not they actually have an advantage over those of us who are free. Have you ever noticed some enter back into the free world with renewed life, energy and an abundance of knowledge? You may not have friends who have been imprisoned, but I have a few. I know far too many from my neighborhood that have been a part of the system. They come out of jail healthier and physically fit compared to the poor or flabby bodies they went in with. They think differently and seem to have gotten wiser. They have had opportunities to educate and develop themselves while locked up.

In a sense, we need to imprison ourselves. We need to separate ourselves from the freedoms of society that hinder our growth. Maybe we should adopt the "Three Hots and a Cot" rule. How good would it do you if you ate breakfast, lunch, and dinner at the same time everyday with no chance of sneaking through the McDonald's drive-thru? How many times do we skip meals because of the hustle and bustle of our lifestyles? We eat on the run, we eat unhealthy, and our portions are at least twice as much as we need. Lights out! What if we went to bed every night at 10:00 p.m. for the next 5-10 years! You probably don't need that much. A year of going to bed early and consistently would definitely add years to your life. We have too many responsibilities or we are putting emphasis on the wrong things in our lives. You have no choice when you're locked up. The lights are going off no matter what. We need to educate ourselves, but we can't 'cause we have jobs, kids, and important things to do with our time. Some prisoners become well versed in Law, religions, economics, government and politics. One of the most knowledgeable people I know received a bachelor's and master's degree inside the confinement of prison walls. You would be amazed at the intelligence gained inside while being rehabilitated. Some, who choose to, develop discipline and have to follow certain honor codes to survive and thrive in their world. Sure, not all prisoners follow that path and some use their knowledge for evil when they get out; but I just want to drive home the fact that we should be imprisoning ourselves in this free world of ours. We should be educating ourselves, getting our square meals a day, and getting proper rest no matter what. It's okay if you imprison yourself for a while. There are some people who have not seen me in some time because I am getting rehabilitated. No longer do I have access to many of the trappings of freedom. This discipline has been self-inflicted.

There are mental bars and imaginary walls that can shelter us from the negatives that can stop our growth. For a percentage of criminals released from prison, it is hard to function outside of those walls. They become IT or institutionalized. Brooks from the movie "Shawshank Redemption" couldn't function as a free man. The freedoms of this world will have you eating whatever you want, doing whatever you want, and they stop you from getting the proper recuperation. You may need a warden to tell you, "lights out!"

"Emancipate yourselves from mental slavery; None but ourselves can free our minds" Bob Marley

Self-deception is one of the biggest roadblocks on the journey to success in any field. We convince ourselves that life is good and that we don't need or want the better things that life has to offer. Our Ego gets in the way of us dealing with reality and the truth. The truth is usually a punch in the face of our ego. Not many people can accept the fact that they are not achieving in life at the level they should be, so they rationalize why they are not in a certain career field, why they are just cruising through life, and why they are not making forward progress. When we really face the truth, we see that there are areas in our lives that we need to work on. It may be the way we talk to others, our self-esteem, attitude, our drive, or even being a good parent or spouse. We tell ourselves that we are good in certain areas, but the scoreboard doesn't seem to show results that match that.

Admitting that there is a problem is the first step in every recovery group out there. We need to recover, but first we must admit to the problem. "My name is Rickey and I have not been leading my family as a good husband and good father should." That is basically how my journey started. I admitted my faults and weaknesses and decided to start working on them.

As you work on changing ways that are less becoming of you, you'll find other areas in your life that need to be addressed.

Yes it hurts to admit that we need help in areas ... that we need to change. It hurts worse to think of the future where the problems we hold within will only get worse. Have you seen others who are so self-deceived that they don't even realize that they are the train wreck that everyone is watching? If you haven't noticed, that person could be you. I've looked in the mirror and not recognized the image before me. I was not proud of that man.

Some people are comfortable with the lies that they are living. Those who are incompetent don't realize how incompetent they are. They have a very difficult time recognizing competency. People think that they are better at things than they really are. It is very difficult to help someone with a problem that you clearly see if the person doesn't see that problem. The teacher can only appear when the student is ready. With that said, change has to start within. We must look at ourselves and evaluate where we are in life. We must be truthful and free of self-deception.

Where does your Self-directed Shift start? You know the answer. We all have the answers and the keys to the lives we want to live. We know exactly what to do. There is no doubt where the starting point is. It is right here. It is right now. It is with me. There is no need to look past who I am right now.

CHAPTER 14

Small Steps of Disciplined Actions

"Discipline is the bridge between goals and accomplishment."

-Jim Rohn

Water is cold at 33 degrees. It is ice, frozen at 32 degrees. At 211 degrees is hot; but at 212 degrees it is boiling. Think about that for a second. The degree of difference is very slight. There is such a little increase one way or the other but the results are drastic. There are slight degrees of separation that often determines success from failure. There are even positive and negative connotations that are divided by slight degrees of difference. In high school, I was not considered fast because I ran a 4.6 second forty-yard dash. A 4.4 meant you were fast! The difference was only two-tenths of a second. When I played baseball, no one thought of you as a hard thrower if you topped-out at 89mph. If you could throw the baseball 90mph, you were considered to have a strong arm. I say all of this to demonstrate or illustrate the slight differences in degrees and the thoughts behind them. There are many more, like the difference between winner and loser of a boxing match. The decision could come down to two or three more punches landed and result in hundreds of thousands of dollars difference between the two.

Success is often determined by those small degrees of difference. What are we doing to create that small degree? You may be working very hard and not getting your desired results. There are three principles you may need to implement into your life. Time management, Self-Improvement and Daily discipline. First of all, are you using your time wisely? Is the work you are doing just busy work, or is it benefiting the priorities in your life? Have you set your priorities for day-to-day activities? You should write down those important must-do tasks every day. Constantly check your list and eliminate those "to do's".

Stop wasting your time. It is the most valuable and precious thing we have. When it's gone, we can't get it back. Have you ever looked back at a day or even a week, thought about how busy you were but realized that you didn't get very much accomplished? Activity and results are two totally different things.

We need to focus on results more, rather than just doing or working. What am I accomplishing? Every morning before I leave the house, I read my resolutions and the last one I read is: Improve-Always Improve. Be better today at everything than I was yesterday. Self-Improvement is the key to my life. It should be a focus of everyone wanting to succeed. The Self-directed Shift is my fountain of youth. It is what has given me new life. I am trying to improve my situation and the lives of everyone around me. Discipline is the harder of the three but the most important. Start disciplining yourself on the very small things in life. They will lead to the big things, which will lead to the small degrees of differences, which separate those who are on top from the rest of the crowd. If you don't discipline yourself, someone else will. It's much easier and more bearable when you are holding the whip.

It's the 4th of July. It's a great day for the Lewis family and many other families around the country. As I woke up this morning, I can't help but think of the fun and awesome food we will eat today. I know I will eat way more barbecue than I should. I may stuff my mouth with cakes and pies just because they will be in front of me. With all that said, this makes a tough discussion. Heart disease and diabetes are killing us more than anything in this world. Sixty-five percent of adults are overweight or obese. Almost forty percent of adults are not even physically active. Let's not even talk about the trend in children and teens! We are dying and it's like we don't even care. We don't care that our kids are dying. We don't really care that we are dying.

We know what foods are good for us and what foods are not. We understand that we need to exercise and that we need to make sure our kids stay active, but we really don't. We are information rich in today's society. There is an abundance of healthy alternatives for eating out there. At the click of a button you can find recipes for great tasting, healthy, foods, desserts and snacks. The social network PINTEREST is a great place to finds ideas. Walking every day is easy to do. Why don't we take the simple steps to ensure our health and the health of our family? It's because of the invisible results. Things that are good and part of healthy living are easy to do, but they are also easy not to do. We choose more often, not to do them. A greasy cheeseburger will not harm you or help you today, but eat them consistently over time and they will kill you. The individual result of eating an unhealthy snack is invisible. Have you ever seen someone have a heart attack or stroke that seemed to be in good health? It was the accumulation of small errors in judgment; 20-30 years of choosing the chips over the apples; sodas over fresh juices and water; driving two blocks instead of walking.

I just got back from running the Bay St. Louis Bridge (2.5miles). You don't have to run a bridge like that. Just start walking. Walk your block. One time! The key is to do it consistently over time. Do it every day or every other day. Make it part of your lifestyle like brushing your teeth. You may not see the results in a week or even a couple of months, but there is a positive result happening. Over time that result will appear so great that others won't believe their eyes. Drink a glass of water as soon as you wake up in the morning, eat an orange every day at lunchtime, have a small salad at every dinner for the rest of your life and watch what happens.

Define the healthy life you want to live. Learn from those with that type of healthy lifestyle. Do what it takes to get those results. Do what they do to get their results. It all starts with our thinking. Read "The Slight Edge" by Jeff Olson. It's one of the best books I've read on simple daily disciplines that can alter your life for the better. Jim Collins, author of "Good to Great", says that success is disciplined people engaging in disciplined thought and conducting disciplined actions. It all starts with our thoughts. The beginning of our Self-directed Shift in discipline starts with our thinking. Everything originates from our head and radiates outward through the manifestation of our actions.

We need to create habits that become a part of who we are. We need habits that transform into lifestyles. The discipline of doing little things or taking small steps towards your goals and dreams becomes easier with time. You only need to do them and do them consistently so that the pain of cracking that whip becomes easier over time and you can get to your desired results.

Van Jones, author of *The Grinder's Guidebook: 12 Steps to Significant and Sustainable Success*, states that extreme discipline is the most important step to achieving and sustaining any success. *"It may not always feel good, taste good, or look good, but if we force ourselves to do the small and seemingly insignificant things that unsuccessful people refuse to do, we will truly benefit in the end."* Nothing can last if you are not a disciplined person. It is imperative to create disciplines in every area of your life to hold on to that which you have worked so hard for. It is so easy to blow months of training with one binge in an area that you are weak. We all fall short or slip from time to time, but truly disciplined people don't allow one piece of chocolate cake to become an all-out feast on desserts at every chance they get. Truly disciplined people don't allow not being able to get to the gym today, to become three months of sitting on the couch and gaining twenty pounds.

If I gave you $100 for every pound you lost in the next 90 days, how many pounds will you lose? What if I gave you one hundred more dollars a day for the rest of your life for maintaining the weight you lost. How long could you keep it off? What if you would receive a new car for truly mending that broken relationship with your father? What kind of car would you be driving? I bet you could get some things accomplished with the right motivation.

We know most of the things we should be doing in life that would be producing maximum benefits, but we just won't apply them. We are not stupid people. You and I both know the effects of overeating, smoking, and drinking. We know that words hurt, yet we still use them in ways that are crippling to our children. We understand that we need to save money and create wealth for a rainy day, but we don't. We just don't have the proper motivation to do what is right.

Motivation can come in the form of losing something or gaining something important to us. It is sad to see people get that motivation when it is almost too late. I say almost because it is never too late. God has the final word on everything. You want to start eating healthy now that you've had a heart attack. The doctor tells you that you have spots on your lungs and now you threw away the Newport's, Marlboro's, Camel's or whatever cigarette brand is killing you. Now you want to do right when she leaves you for that guy down the street. We call him Jody. He's the one who's disciplined and does the little things consistently. Now Jody has got you buying flowers and paying attention to your Love. Motivation needs to be applied in every area of your life in the form of rewards. You must set checkpoints, goals, and targets in your life and then pay yourself for doing what you accomplished. That keeps you going. We should be constantly setting benchmarks and attaching rewards, but those rewards can't be counterproductive. If I lose 20lbs, I will treat myself to cake and ice cream. That's not good. Apply it to your situation. Start small. Everyone can do better. Everyone likes being rewarded. Make your reward your motivation to get the things you want out of life. Treat yourself to a movie only when you hit that 20lb weight loss goal. Stop eating your favorite food until you can make it to work on time for 30 days in a row. Reward yourself by "sleeping in" one Saturday for hitting some financial goal you have. I'm just giving some generalities. Start today. Figure out what you want and attach your motivation.

What's the best way to skin a cat? Doesn't matter. Just skin him! I get asked a lot of questions on how to do something. Which way should I do this? There are multiple ways and some ways are better than others. But if indecision is causing you not to do anything, you're going backwards. You are losing time, your most precious resource. Just do the thing. So what if it is wrong. So what if it is not as good as it could be. Do it, and then make corrections. Do it; then do it again. You have to decide to take a step forward and put one foot in front of the other and walk. That is progress even if the direction is slightly off. Standing still on any decision is moving backwards because the world is constantly moving. Time stands still for no man. Even if you wait, you can't just one day take off as fast as you can and think everything is going to be okay. Going faster when you're late causes problems. Some will never even take off, even if they say they will. You will never get back the time you took twiddling your thumbs. Today, stop talking about it, stop thinking about the task, stop asking how and just get the sharpest knife (you have) and skin the cat. You have to be disciplined enough to move forward. Take action even when it may not be known what the best action is.

CHAPTER 15

Character & Integrity

"Honesty and integrity are absolutely essential for success in life - all areas of life. The really good news is that anyone can develop both honesty and integrity."

-Zig Ziglar

You may be a person of good character. I'm sure that you can name a handful of other persons who you would describe as having character. What about integrity? How many people do you know with integrity? I searched Google and Wikipedia for the definitions of those words and they all were pretty much the same everywhere I looked. Both definitions describe strong moral principles, honesty and upstanding values. As I looked deeper and searched for deeper meanings, I discovered what separates the two. It's action.

I see students every year that come through my classes with good character. Some, I would say, have great character, but are lacking integrity. They do the right thing. Follow all of the rules and stay on the right side of the road. When others are doing wrong, participating in questionable acts, and making immoral judgments, they do nothing. Let's say there's a classroom of twenty students. Ten of those students are bullying and picking on one student for being overweight. The remainder of the students are of good character and will not be a part of the foolishness. They would never make fun of another person or participate in anything like that, so they turn their heads. Every now and then you will find a student out of the bunch with integrity. That student stands up against wrong. Integrity is pushing character into action. Someone who not only doesn't participate in actions that are immoral, illegal, or unethical, but stands against those who do. Integrity is fighting for what is right. Integrity is going against the crowd when the crowd is wrong. Are you a person of integrity? Is there action in your character? Do you turn your head when others are doing wrong because it's not your business? I've been building my character my whole life. Now I'm working on my integrity.

When you start shifting in your life from the path that most are taking, unexpected joy from your decisions and actions start to radiate from within your soul. Elevating your character and integrity produces feelings outside of what you would normally expect. We don't always do the right thing and often that never bothers us. We have been doing the wrong things for so long that it becomes normal and has no effect on our conscience.

As I look back over the financial impact of our recent vacation, I see where a few years ago we would have saved much more money but at the expense of my family's integrity. I grew up with the "hook up" or getting over whenever I could. Many of us have no problem with telling a little white lie to save a penny or two. It may not be a big deal to you to falsify a document so that your children can get free or reduced lunch. Maybe to you it's okay if the clerk at the grocery store forgets to charge you for an item. After all, it's not going to hurt Wal-Mart if I get by with one extra item that the associate forgot to scan. It's their fault right? Wrong! As I grow and develop my character and build solid integrity, it becomes increasingly hard to do the little things that have been a norm my whole life. I now see them as infractions on who I am.

We could have saved over $100 on our vacation at restaurants and attractions by simply stating that my young children were younger than they actually were. I know many people do this. Even some seniors age themselves by a couple of years to get half off on their breakfast or a free coffee. We do a lot of those seemingly harmless, little actions that are actually rotting away our character and drilling holes in the integrity that is supposed to give us our honor.

On day one of the trip, I was struck with the dilemma of lying to save $8.00 or hold on to a precious part of my soul. A couple of years before, maybe even a couple of months earlier, I would have saved those $8.00. I didn't tell that little white lie and it made me feel proud to do the right thing. Making the right choice on such a small scale is much more rewarding to me than when my character is put to the test on large issues. There is no dilemma there. Every day I had the choice to lie and save money or tell the truth and save myself. Every day it got easier and easier to display my character and integrity in front of my family and myself. What would it have done to my boys if they would've heard me lie about their ages to save money? I can't take those chances anymore. I can't judge you for doing the things that I no longer do. I can't condemn you for the choices you make that I have made in the past. I am not perfect and neither is any man walking this earth. I have many issues that I am working on and flaws that I am trying to correct. I only urge you to do the right thing because it's the right thing.

I've been lied to my whole life. More than likely you have also. Some were supposedly to protect me -- small lies, or little white lies. Some lies are traditional, like the Tooth Fairy and Santa Claus. Some were huge, big deals that have left lasting impacts and built the structure of some of the relationships I have. Others have torn down the structures that were once solid. Some people have told me lies and don't even know that I know the truth, so they continue and add more lies to cover the previous. The worst I've been hurt in my life has not been by intentional physical or verbal assaults but by lies of someone intentionally deceiving to protect themselves or supposedly to protect me.

The most harm I've done to someone else is when I have done that exact thing. Told a lie. As a kid, I was relieved to find out that there was no Santa, but at the same time I was really hurt because it was the first realization that my mother had lied to me and kept that lie for years. That was just the tale of a fictional character. Imagine the impact of more serious issues on the human psyche. There is a reason why "Thou shall not lie" is one of God's laws. Big or small, a lie can destroy so much. It creates a ripple effect of destruction that may not be seen until too late. A lie is a hole in a person's character and integrity. Often the effects are irreversible, or the character of the liar may never be repaired in the eyes of the ones being lied to. Let's tell the truth even when it's hard to do so. Even if it is uncomfortable and brings pain to the ears of those who have to hear the truth, that pain will not compare to the pain of a lie manifested over time when the truth is eventually revealed. The Self-directed Shift that starts with our thinking also starts with truths. We must not lie to others and we must be truthful with ourselves.

I didn't even ask for it! There was no reason for him to tell it to me. When was the last time you told a lie? Think about it. Some of us have to think back further than others. Some of us may have just lied today. I just want to pose a few questions. Why do we lie? Is there ever a good reason? Does it bother you to tell a lie, or is it just part of life? Is there such a thing as a little white lie? Can they really be small and harmless? Often parents lie to protect their children. Is it the child being protected or is it the parent protecting himself or herself from the plight of explaining the truth?

Often, we don't forget when someone lies to us. No matter the reason, you expose your ability to lie. The possibility of you lying will be in the minds of others. Will you only lie in certain situations, for certain reasons, or to certain people? I will only lie to my boss when I don't want to go in to work. That's okay! Everyone does that, right? Maybe that's not okay. Of course one lie leads to another and you have to protect one lie with the next. When do you stop? The problem comes when our lies are exposed. How do you feel when you realize that a person has found out about your lie? Do you deny til death? Does it hurt? How do you feel when your mother finds out or your brother catches you telling a big one? How do you feel when a person dear to your heart has betrayed you with a lie? Maybe no one has ever told you that they know you lied. Your friends, family, and even strangers are smarter than you think.

No matter how good you are, no matter how well you tell your story, someone knows that you are lying and they may be letting you continue to dig yourself deeper into a twisted web of lies and untruths. One of the most important ingredients of a healthy relationship is trust. When trust is gone, because of lies, everything you say and do is questioned. Build strong character. Gain the trust of others. Tell the truth no matter the situation. Develop an inability to lie. Even when it doesn't seem to matter, be straight with the next person. You don't have to make yourself seem "bigger" than you are. It really doesn't matter what others think about the truth. It is the truth! That lie you told me isn't just between you and me. It's between you and God. Mark Twain said it best, "If you tell the truth, you don't have to remember anything."

Our reputation will get us far in life or it can hinder our progress. It is what others think of us. Character is who we really are. Usually they are aligned, but sometimes there is a disconnect between the two. We must work to keep them on the same plane.

Lies are detrimental, so how important is the truth? Many of us live inside of lies and we have no problem with them. They are all we know. The lies, misconceptions, and falsehoods have built the facades of the life we live. The truth is the truth. Do you really want to hear it, is the question? Many people don't really want to hear it. I was one of those people, because the truth exposes who you are and what you are doing in your life. We don't want a paradigm shift in our thinking because we are comfortable where we are and with what we believe regardless of its validity. There may be something in your life that you know is not right. It may be tradition or something you were just born into. You may not want to hear the truth because it will cause you to change your thinking or your actions and change is a difficult thing.

Being wrong is not a problem for us. Realizing that we are wrong is what brings the pain. I use to spare other's feelings when I knew that they were wrong. I was not always a truth teller. I didn't lie; I just opted to allow those people to continue to wear a veil over their eyes. In some cases, I wore that very same veil by choice. It's the RED or BLUE pill scenario. Subconsciously, we choose to steer clear of the truth because accepting the truth usually means we have to do something different than what we are doing.

On this journey of ours, the tables start shifting. We must look inside ourselves and find the tact to convey the truth to others without damaging the sensitivity of the human spirit. I hurt others. I do not do so intentionally. I only tell the truth with the intent of them learning and growing through new information. Some people don't want to hear what I have to say; not because it's not true or that I'm rude. They won't want to hear you either. It's because they already know the truth and it hurts when it's put in their face.

The truth often rips at our character, discipline and integrity. It cripples us because we have been held up by false information and facades that allow us to drift through life not living up to our potential or achieving the things we once truly desired. The truth is a blow to the head. It's a knife in the gut or a bullet in the heart and the person delivering that truth becomes the assailant of the crime. I am sorry for your pain but I don't apologize for giving you what you need. The Truth. I apologize for not being more sensitive to your struggle. At one point I wore those same shoes and carried the same crosses. At this time in your life, you may not want to hear the truth. You may just want a friend. A true friend knows when to give you the truth or not allow you to hear it.

He was looking for some sympathy, but deep down I knew he needed to hear what I was about to share. He's sixteen years old and the words that came out his mouth lit a fire underneath me even if he was just looking for a little love. I love my job as a high school teacher and the teachable moments it provides on a daily basis. "It doesn't matter what I do. No one cares or pays attention to me. Why should I always do what's right if it's not going to make a difference?"

Quickly I jumped on my soapbox and started. Don't talk like that! What you do does matter. No matter what it is, your actions will affect people and you may not even know it; your good actions as well as your bad ones. People are watching and feeding off of your every step. There is information being transmitted by each move you make. You need to be a force for good. There are enough people out there doing things that are not so good. You are young and don't understand how much power you have. There are people who are twice as old as you who don't understand their power. You have the power to save lives or kill dreams by simple actions. Imagine if you harnessed that power for good. Someone could be having a horrible day that can be turned around by something as simple as your smile because you sensed that they were feeling blue. What you do matters. What you say matters. Train yourself in doing the right thing always because it's the right thing. The result might be seemingly insignificant to you but you don't always see the results when the door closes or the person walks away. You may not have seen the little kid who looks up to you, watching from around the corner.

By our nature, negative acts, thoughts and feelings are more likely to be duplicated, so how about eliminating those negative things from your life. What you do matters because you matter. You have purpose and that purpose is good. What if you constantly do what is right? It will rub off on others and those persons' actions will rub off on even more people. Soon your small little acts become huge because they are replicated on a scale larger than you could imagine. I ended the conversation with this: "You matter. Look at me and listen carefully. If you didn't matter, you wouldn't be here. You are going to make a difference. You are going to affect the lives of everyone you come in contact with in some shape, form, or fashion. It will be positive or negative, but the choice is yours to make." As I finished the talk with the young man, I realized that I was re-educating myself and realizing the gravity of the number of lives that cross my path. Am I always doing what's right? I know what I do matters. Am I being a force for good? Are you being a force for good? Be the change and take the actions for others to follow. You matter. We all matter.

At some point you need to set your selfish ways aside. You may now belong to something bigger than just you. You belong to a unit, a group, a family, a team or a community. What's best for you as an individual may not be best for the entity that you are a part of.

Every year as a baseball coach, I tried to explain this concept to my team. You may be the best shortstop on this team. I may know it. You, your parents, and the rest of the world may know it, but you may never play that position. It may be in your best interest to play shortstop, but not in the best interest of the team as a whole. You may have to play first base, because no one else can play that position. The puzzle just may fit better with you somewhere you might not have imagined you would be. It's hard to give up your individual goals and dreams and adopt those of the unit you belong to. The group takes priority over the individual. The question is this. Do you sacrifice yourself for the benefit of others? One of the hardest things to do is to go against what would benefit you the most and go with what will benefit the group more. Would you vote for something that would only benefit 20% of the people involved because you are part of that 20%? Would you vote for the other thing that would benefit 80% of the people involved although you belong to the other 20%? That is a tough decision that we have to make. Self-preservation is a hard concept to break. There are five people on the boat and it's going to sink. You all will die unless one of you sacrifices themselves and jumps so that the other four can live. Would you give your life so that others can live? That is much deeper of a thought. Would you do it for your children? Would you do it for your wife or husband? What about a friend? Would you sacrifice a vote that would save you, for one that would save a larger group? Would you do it in your church? What about in your community? Would you sacrifice for the benefit of your country?

The best thing to do is find a way that everyone involved benefits the most with minimal collateral damage, but we all know that eggs have to be broken to make omelets and not all people can be happy. Someone will have to fall on the sword for the benefit of others. Are you the type of person who always looks out for himself, or can you put your prosperity on the shelf in order for the unit to benefit? Remember, you belong to something bigger than just you.

CHAPTER 16

Find Your Purpose & Leave a Legacy

"Purpose is when you know and understand what you were born to accomplish. Vision is when you see it in your mind and begin to imagine it."

-Myles Munroe

Each one of us has unique gifts and talents that have been put inside of us. Many have undiscovered abilities that could possibly blossom into something meaningful and fulfilling. I see people every day walking around and going about living their lives miserable and unhappy. They do not understand that they control the outcome of their true happiness. Many are not doing on a daily basis the things, which they were created, to do or uncovering those special talents and participating in the active process of creating their happiness through their gifts. I understand the cruel world that we live in. I know you see no other way right now but to work this dead-end job, be a slave to the only system you know, and concede to the idea that "this is the way the cookie crumbles".

There is a better way of life that you can live. It comes from within you. The seeds of great fruit have already been planted inside of each and every one of us. They simply need to be watered. Discover your passions and your purpose. Discover that which makes you happy. There is something inside of you that desperately wants to come out, but may have been suppressed by the false sense of security of working at things outside of your purpose. If creativity lies within you, what are you doing that employs that creativity? Maybe your passion centers around food, but you don't work in the food industry or have very much time and resources to cook at home. This is where your unhappiness and meager living comes from.

The further you are away from your passions and purpose, the further you are away from the meaningful existence and abundantly joyful life available to you. Your purpose in life is to find your purpose in life, and do everything you can towards fulfilling that purpose.

Great debaters have wrestled with this question. Philosophers, scientists, the religious, spiritual believers and non-believers alike have struggled to come up with a definitive answer. What is the purpose of life? If you asked one million people that very question, it is quite possible that you would get one million different answers. As open-minded as I try to be, I can't conceive of the idea that there is no purpose in life, but there are millions who believe that there isn't. It may be very hard for you and me to put our finger on the meaning and purpose of life, but we will try to explain and give our opinion if asked.

Usually we will answer with something deep and meaningful ... something that would probably go nicely on the inside of a Hallmark card. We may not even believe our own words. Something easier to discover than the purpose of life in general is the purpose of your life. What is your purpose? If you don't have a clue, I will tell you as I've said before. Your purpose is to find your purpose. You must be actively engaged in the process of figuring out who you are and what you are supposed to be doing. If it takes your whole life, so be it.

There is a reason you are here. There is a reason you are reading these words. Everything has a purpose. Your purpose is to find your purpose and develop it with all of your heart. I can't say that enough times. When you find your purpose you will do it for free. I would pay people to listen to me if I had to.

Teaching/educating is the one thing that gets me fired up! My purpose is to educate the uninformed and the misinformed through life-changing information. It has brought me to a place where I educate inside of a classroom and on the streets with every person who's looking for a better way. I've found my purpose ... or my purpose for now. I've found one of many things that I know I was meant to do. I was lost with no direction until I searched for my purpose. Have you found yours? You won't if you aren't looking. And if you are looking, there's still no guarantee you will find it. Your purpose may be the search itself because that will be what carries you successfully through life.

As you search for your purpose, you will no longer feel like a piece of driftwood floating along in the rough rapids of a wild river. You will become like a mighty sea vessel piloted by a great explorer looking for a new world among the seven seas. Get in your boat and discover new land. Discover your purpose. At least, set sail and enjoy the adventure.

I see students year in and year out who have no direction or purpose. They have not a clue as to what paths to take in life. Even worse is seeing adults living the same way. If you're not moving forward, you're moving backwards. If you aren't going up, you're going down. You are either on a positive track moving in a positive direction or the opposite. You will never find your purpose if you don't start moving forward, up and positive. Start with your dreams and with what you love. Turn over every rock. Look around every corner and behind every door until you find it.

We are living our lives on accident or by a series of coincidences. How many of us out there are doing what we what to do? How many of us are living the life we always wanted? I asked a series of questions to my students:

How many of you would like to work as a cocktail waitress, work at a gas station, cut grass for a living, deliver pizzas for Dominos, or work at the local concrete processing plant? No hands went up. No one had dreams to do any of those jobs. I'm not saying that there is anything wrong with those jobs if that is what you want. The problem many of us face is that we accidently fall into those jobs.

Years of teaching have shown me bright and talented kids with drive and purpose that go off to college and lose sight of their purpose and dreams. Within a year or two, they fall into those "not-so dream" careers and they rationalize why didn't because a doctor, lawyer or whatever that they had envisioned for so long. So many people will wake up one day with a wrinkled face and brittle bones and they would have not lived their lives with a purpose. What is it that inspires you? Stop living by accident. Find your purpose! Do, and get the things you want out of life.

Everyone has a purpose but so many don't have vision. They just haven't found it yet. Those students every year who have not a clue of what to do in life fall for any and everything. It's not their fault. It's not entirely your fault that you are just floating down stream like driftwood with no direction. Someone at some point has to encourage you and cultivate the seed inside of you so that you can continue to water your purpose to make it grow. My purpose, or a major part of the purpose of my life, is to educate the ignorant. I do not mean that in any derogatory sense. We just don't know what we don't know. I've been educating those who lack knowledge or awareness my entire life. Naturally I became a teacher, but by educating the ignorant I'm not limited to a classroom. Do you have to be a classroom teacher if this is your purpose? No. I won't be in the classroom forever; but I will forever be educating those in need and those who want to be educated.

There are people out there seeking, looking for their purpose and trying to find their meaning. Everyone has a purpose. Your purpose in life is to find your purpose and then submit to its will. Have I said that before? The thing that we must all realize is that our purpose is in us, but it is not entirely for us. Your purpose will be tied to you serving others. It is very much like making someone happy and you consequently becoming happy. You will benefit from your purpose as a by-product of serving others. To find your purpose, find out who needs what you have to give. Maybe your purpose will lie in one of these areas: Heal the sick, feed the hungry, liberate the captive, educate the ignorant, heal families, spread prosperity, or something along those lines.

There are many purposes out there that are inside of each one of us. Detect what is already in you by asking the question "what do I have to offer others?" How can I serve others? Oliver De Mille, author of the book "A Thomas Jefferson Education" states that we should see the world as it is, see the world as it should be, and place ourselves between them so that we can push towards the way it should be. Make a difference. How do you serve others? What would you do to serve others that you would do without being paid to do it? Profit will come as something secondary to the drive of you fulfilling your potential, which is catapulted by your passion. Each one of us was created with talents and gifts planted deep inside of us that are to be shared with the world and used as acts of service.

Where is the richest place on earth? Many would say in the oil fields of the Middle East, the diamond mines of Africa, or any distant land full of natural resources that the world desires. As most of the world would answer, most will be wrong. The richest place on earth is the cemetery. Right now I want you to think about all of the dreams and goals that you have yet to accomplish. Think about the business you want to start up, the books you want to write, the investments you want to make, the record deal you want to sign, the television shows you want to produce, and the Broadway plays you want to act in. Now multiply that by the millions upon millions of people just like you with extraordinary talents who never do anything about it. Those talents and the potential for greatness are buried in the ground for all the world not to see. There are Presidents, Senators, and Mayors who will never take office. There will be doctors, surgeons, and nurses who will never get a chance to provide their services because the ability to become just that will die as an unfulfilled dream of a person who fails to find their purpose. If you died right now, what dreams, ideas, talents and abilities will die with you? We must die empty. What is your use to the world and to yourself dying full? Each one of us is full with greatness, but greatness rarely comes out.

Today is a sad day for all of your friends and family. It is the day of your funeral and it's sad that you have left us so early. Some believe it wasn't your time to go because you were so young. Others believe that it was God's will to bring you home to the "Upper Room". You have lived your life and it's over now. Your kids are crying. Your parents are crying. Your friends also cry as some sit and some stand in their nice suits and fancy funeral dresses. Someone has brought fried chicken and your great aunt made red beans for the repast. But before everyone can stuff their faces with potato salad and gumbo, someone has to speak kind words over the top of your body, as you lay motionless in that shiny new metallic coffin. They will have to tell the story of your life.

Someone has to speak highly of the accomplishments of your life, your character, and what you meant to the world while you were alive. Will that be a hard task? Will the truth have to be stretched for the sake of respect for you and your family? What will people say outside of the church when not many people are listening? Will anyone be talking at all?

If you are reading this, today isn't really your funeral day, right? No, but that day will come. That day will come for all of us. What legacy will you leave? What will your friends really be saying about you when you can't answer back? What will your children or parents say about you? If people are honest, they may not have very much positive to say about your life and all of your accomplishments or who you were as a person. You must decide what you want the preacher, priest, or rabbi to say about you. You must decide what type of speeches will come out of the mouths of your friends and family. Whatever you want them to say, go out and make it happen. Be the things you want others to remember you for. It's not too late.

I don't want to be known for being a good baseball player or someone who took his life for granted. I'm working on my character, my integrity, and my purpose in life. Will you be known for something less superficial than being a good cake decorator, having nice cars, or being the best line dancer in the club? The condition that you are at right now does not have to be your final state.

In the small town of Bessemer, AL, there is already a gravestone that bears the name, Rickey Lewis. There is a date to which he was born and a date to which he passed. None of us are immune to the same fate. At some point in the history of this world, more than likely in a small town in Mississippi, there will be another gravestone that will bear that same name with different dates. One thing that will appear the same and the same on every other person of this world's grave will be that little dash between those numbers. They will all look alike, but they all will have different meanings.

What will your dash stand for? What will it represent? In Fr. Larry Richards' book, "Be A Man", he writes in chapter 1, "You are going to die. This is the truest reality there is. This is what makes us all the same. "What a way to start off a book that is meant to encourage! He, along with Stephen R. Covey, reminds us to begin with the end in mind and then we can focus our energy on our path. My dash has become much more important than the born-on date that I celebrate year after year. It is the legacy we will leave, the good we have done, and our impact on the world and others. With a little Google search you will find the NBA draft status of the first Rickey Lewis in 1976 and you can even find the MLB draft status of me, the second Rickey Lewis in 1998. I loved the idea of my father, but I can count the number of times I've seen him in my life. He was a legend, and still is, in the small towns of the South. Many have great stories regarding his ability to play the game of basketball; but I seldom hear stories of how good of a father he was, how good of a husband, or his service and sacrifice for others. I'm sure there are a number of people who would speak highly of him in a variety of ways; but his legacy -- his dash -- was his athletic achievements. As much as I love sports, I don't want to be known for how well I threw a baseball or my impact on the football field in college.

That dash is who you are, what you have accomplished and contributed to society. That dash is what will live forever. That dash should be made up of character, integrity, responsibility, trustworthiness, service, sacrifice, and a host of other words that play into the dynamic make-up of a man doing more than just existing between those dates. It should be a glorious journey. Ask yourself every day -- what can I do to serve others? How can I be an impact on someone's life today in a positive uplifting way? How will others describe your dash?

Legacy. What does that word mean to you? It may mean the forty-four points you scored in the district championship basketball game at your high school. Your legacy may be the stories of your glory days as a track star, a playground bully, the best dancer ever to wear a pair of dancing shoes, or any of your talents and abilities that won't fade so quickly with time. A monument, a statue, or a dedicated building may define a legacy. My legacy will manifest in my three sons. It won't be just the fact that they are biologically mine, and my legacy will not be limited to them and my subsequent bloodlines. Our true legacy is in the people we impact with our purpose that carry on parts of our purpose and missions in life as their own after we are gone. When your purpose outruns you, then and only then have you created your legacy. All of the things that I care about and all that I am will always live on. I know that others out there will take with them parts of my passion and purpose far beyond my existence as I have done with my father and mentor, Armand Francis Theriault, SVD. My legacy only starts with my sons and will grow from all those who listen and appreciate my purpose.

My purpose is to educate and become a person of influence. I will be a beacon of light, an example for others to follow. The Lewis boys will shine as the illustrations of right and set the precedent of leading by example. I may not see the fruits of four or five generations of my purpose or mission in life, but it will last as long as this world stands. I am creating my legacy. Will you have a legacy? Are you purposely influencing your great, great, great, grand children by what you are doing today? Father Theriault had no biological children, but he raised and influenced hundreds. A couple hundred years from now, his name and mine may disappear forever but our actions and the residual results will last forever. Create a better you, find your purpose, leave a true legacy by influencing others, and create a better future for all who will inherit the land we leave behind.

It's harder to build an empire from scratch than having one that was passed down to you. When I was a kid, I was fortunate in being able to play baseball with the "rich kids" because my mother missed the sign-up date for the city league. I was forced to play with the affluent kids, who happened to be mostly white, from the other side of town rather than the black kids from the projects I lived in and went to school with.

That event when I was nine started a chain reaction that led to me wanting more and being drafted into professional baseball when I was twenty-one years old. I got a great opportunity to see how kids my age, who had money, lived their ordinary lives. It was far from ordinary to me. They had their own swimming pools in the backyards of their huge houses that had garages with multiple new cars. They had grass! They had real grass growing on American soil that belonged to them. I have watched those types of kids take an easier path in life. I watch it in the students I teach, who drive nicer cars than those in the teachers' parking lot.

There are already mini empires established that are being handed down from one generation to the next. I was not handed the empire of my parents' fortunes. There was no car given to me at sixteen; there was no college tuition money set aside for me to get an education; and there was certainly no trust fund for me to start my life out on the right foot when I turned twenty-one. There is no company that my father has left for me to run or take over after he retired. There wasn't any family land, property or assets that was passed to me. When my father died, there was no insurance policy that came to my brother and me. There is no empire, big or small. I have to create it. Big or small, there has to be something for me to pass along to my children. I must be able to provide a path for them that the wealthy provide for their children to ensure the highest probability of survival and success. It's not just material, although possessions are important. An empire of knowledge is a huge key to their success. Success is part of the legacy I want to pass along. I must build that empire myself in order to pass it down. Because I was not given an empire to pass along, I have to study the empires of others in order to create one that I can entrust to my children for their children and their children's children to benefit. True wealth is passed down from generation to generation. This is true for all types of wealth. If you have not been given an empire, it is your duty to create one, no matter how hard it may be. Leave more than your hat. Pass down more than your brown eyes and gap teeth.

CHAPTER 17

An Attitude of Gratitude

"Be thankful for what you have; you'll end up having more. If you concentrate on what you don't have, you will never, ever have enough."

-Oprah Winfrey

Our world is so small. We live on a planet with about seven billion other human beings; but how many do we interact with? How many are in our state, city or community? There's not many in comparison to the number of people walking this beautiful planet.

I know what you're going through is bad. I know it's tough and almost unbearable. I know you feel lonely and you don't think anyone one cares or understands. I do. Someone else does. Your problems were not invented today. Someone out there just like you is going through the same situation and many have it a lot worse. I do not wish to make light of your situation. It is a big deal because it may be the biggest thing you have had to deal with in your life. It may be the biggest issue you may ever face. I just hope that you can come to the realization that it could be much worse. It may not seem like it at the present time but you have so much to be thankful for.

There are people, living breathing human beings, walking this earth that would trade your pain for theirs. They would trade the rest of their life for just one week or even a day of your life. Don't think that you are the only person struggling with this situation. You will get through it. Many have, and this too shall pass. There is relief and greatness that lies ahead. It all starts with the belief that what you are going through is not the end of the world. It is not the worst thing to happen to a person even though it may be the worst thing that has happened to you. I feel your pain. I've been there. You feel like you can't do anything right. Everything goes wrong. When it rains, it pours. You can't catch a break. Bad news after bad news keeps coming your way. Your heart feels like it's in a million pieces. Your mind can't stop wondering. The fear of everything piles on top of each other. You want relief but it is nowhere in sight. It all will pass. I promise. God promises! Believe in that.

Stop listening to the negative thoughts in your head. Start talking to your self. Start believing that you will get through it. Tell yourself that God has a plan to see you through this. Write it on your hand and read it 100 times a day if you have to. There is a reason you are reading these words right now. It is all part of the plan. Are you a thankful person? Even with the problems you are having, there is so much you can be thankful for. You just have to think about them and put those thoughts in your head to overshadow the rest of the heartache. Be thankful for the things that so many people across the globe do not have. Imagine the things that some people don't have like clean running water, shoes on their feet, a roof over their head, medicine, food, an education, or a hospital to give birth in or be born in. Be thankful that you can push a button and set the temperature to 70 degrees when you're hot or 85 when you're cold. You don't have to gather wood and start a fire. You don't have to catch your food or grow a garden. You can pick up a phone and in 30 minutes or less a pizza will show up. We have no idea of the magnitude of problems and conditions that millions of people are going through every day. What do I have to complain about? I can lose everything; all of my material possessions, be heartbroken, and sick. I would still live better than half of the people on this planet. Someone somewhere is dying a painful death right now. You are reading these words and up until a couple of moments ago were thinking that you had it bad. You are on top of the soil breathing. That's a great start to the rest of your life.

I give you the "TEN-TIMES RULE" as part of your Self-directed Shift. We are so close to our problems. We stand face-to-face to the situations. We are mere inches away from all that grief and pain. It may be easy to say and hard to do, but we need to step back. Get out of the zone and away from the blast radius. We almost always overestimate the magnitude of the situations, problems and pains that we go through. We underestimate how good we have it. That's because we allow ourselves to stay trapped in the small bubble of our tiny world that we have created. If you can step back, you would see from a worldview that your problem is not that big of a problem after all.

We don't truly know the struggle of others because we are self-centered. The world seems to revolve around us. It doesn't. That's only our view, which to many, is the only view and perspective that matters. I have just about mastered the "TEN-TIMES RULE". Every time I get sad, upset or even angry at my situation, I think about the people who have it ten times as bad. When I am down because I am broke and can't buy that new thing I want, I think about the people who are ten times as broke as I am. When I'm sick I know that there are others ten times as sick as I am. There are people with ten times the magnitude of the problems you are facing right now. Back away and don't let those things get so close to you. You have it so much better than millions of human beings walking this earth.

When I mentor and counsel teenagers, I try to explain that they are hurt by these teen problems because their world is so small. They feel genuine pain that they see no end to. Years later they would wish they could trade their adult problems for those problems they had as teens. Today I laugh at some of the things that almost "destroyed" my teenage life. As we age, our world becomes bigger and the problems reduce in size. As adults, we stop expanding our worldview and allow our problems to take on a much larger persona. Someone has it ten times worse. There is always someone who will trade your problems for theirs. It's not as bad as it seems right now. Today or the next time you are down and out about a particular circumstance, think about the "TEN-TIMES RULE", pray for those people, and be thankful because you are ten times better off than you thought. It could be worse.

You are not alone. There is a struggle that is eating away at the energy we use and need to function on a day-to-day basis. The struggles become a part of us. We are often consumed with financial, personal, family and health struggles. It seems that as soon as we get a handle on one issue, another one arises. Your struggles are not new. Those financial problems that you are having are not some new occurrence never before seen. The struggles that you are having with your parents or children have been going on since the beginning of time. There are no new problems out there. Someone knows the way out of that dark tunnel that you have found yourself in.

Experience is the best teacher, but it doesn't have to be your experience. The wise man learns from others' mistakes. You can learn from those who have walked that road before you. Follow the footsteps of those who have already struggled and found their way through that struggle to victory. Take your struggle and not just accept it as a tough time in your life. Tackle it. Give all of your energy towards the fight to eliminate that struggle. Utilize others' experiences. Seek wise counsel in the matter at hand. Don't go at it alone. Someone is willing to help you because they know the pain of your struggle.

Our human spirit does not want others to suffer from the things we have suffered from, if it is not necessary. Your struggles may seem to be unbearable, but they are not. They may seem to be as big as anything you have ever experienced, but they probably are small in comparison to the struggles of others around the world. They are definitely manageable and can be defeated. Embrace that struggle. Find someone who has been through it, or learn from others who have published their battles in good life-changing books. Your struggles are just phases that you can get through and survive.

We live life in phases. Never let a phase define you. Whatever is going on in your life, it's just a phase. Don't get attached to your phases, good or bad. Enjoy your phases, but don't become them. So many of us ride so high because of a good job or whatever. We brag on how well we got it. We become something that is only a phase. Nothing lasts forever. Your problems are not going to last forever. If you're not married, broke, sick, heartbroken, don't worry. Maybe you are lost. Don't worry. It's just a phase. Your best phases are ahead of you. Don't let your past phases interfere with your future ones. I can't say it enough. No phase is forever. Think back on your life so far. There is no phase that has lasted the entirety of your existence. If there is something that has lasted a long time so far, it will change. It's still a phase. It may be a long phase but it's still a phase. Nothing lasts forever. I thought that I would play baseball forever. I thought I would coach baseball forever. They were just phases. I never wanted to leave them. God moved me from that phase of my life to a better one. Never would I have thought that life without baseball would be good. God moves us to great if we can only get out of our own way and let Him work. We are on to greater phases and none are forever!

Leave your past in the past. Once you have come out of that phase, use it as a historical reference. Learn from it and move on. The past will only have the life we give it. If you want it to die, if you need it to die, kill it by putting it away and looking forward to your future phase. There may be an old job, a past vice, or even people that you need to let go. Yes! Let them go. There's no room ahead.

We are moving forward and thinking of our blessings. Surely you have plenty to be thankful for. Day after day, I hear complaints of people wanting more out of life. We are constantly being bombarded with negative news and negative attitudes from friends and associates. Maybe it's because we become immune to the good things in our life. I can come home and my wife is preparing a wonderful meal on the stove and in the oven. The aroma fills the air and brightens my eyes. "Man, that smells good!" My attitude has been vitalized and the goodness I feel is immense. What happens in the next hour is exactly what happens in many people's lives. That wonderful aroma fades away. So we think. The smell does not dissipate. We become used to it or immune to the very thing that gave us the joy in the first place.

I noticed something the other day. When I re-entered the house after taking out the trash, my senses were once again invigorated with the fragrance of that home-cooked meal. We lose sight of what we have and complain about what we don't have. Often, we must be reminded of the goodness that God has already provided us with. We may just need to step outside for a minute, come back in, and appreciate our blessings. Be thankful and grateful for those good relationships, the health, the job, the kids, the parents, the finances, the positive associations, and the grace of God. We often don't realize what we had until it's gone. When we start an attitude of gratitude, then and only then are we provided with abundance. God will not put more into your life until you take care of and show appreciation for that which He has already given. It's okay to ask for more and to seek better results in your life, but take a good whiff of what's already cooking in your kitchen. Life is grand!

CHAPTER 18

The Mind

"Man's mind once stretched by a new idea, never regains its original dimension."

-Oliver Wendell Holmes

The human mind is the only part of our being that separates us from every other creature walking the face of this earth. Every other animal thrives off of pure instinct. We mainly act out of choice and decision. Even when we think that we have no choice, we are still choosing our actions. Just how powerful is our mind? In most accounts from scientists and specialists that study the brain, we use only a slight portion of our brain. The highest percentages quoted are about 6-10 percent. Think about your life and all that you have an accomplished. Contribute that to using only the slightest amount of your brain's power. The human mind is a problem-solving machine even at only 6% operational. I'm not to be ugly but, we all must know someone potentially not using 3%. Of course there are exceptions, and some may be using more.

There are some really great thinkers and problem-solvers in this world. Your value in this world to your family, your job and to others is your ability to solve problems. People who make the most on any job are the ones who solve the most problems. Solving problems is bridging the gap between where you are now and the solution that is somewhere in the future. Successful people have just as many problems if not more than people who are not successful. They solve the problems that others don't even want to deal with.

Name a problem you have and I can guarantee that there are millions of people with the same problem. Some will solve their problem and others will succumb to it. I see so many people -- especially some of my students -- who look at problems as permanent roadblocks instead of challenges. Successful people welcome problems to solve. They are thinkers. Less successful people often don't think. They react. They develop habits that gain them some successes. They'll memorize the directions needed to accomplish a task, but not think about the task. Most of them will turn to others for the answers to problems, which is okay if you just want the answers that someone else has figured. You can tap and harness the power of your own mind. Just as you work out to build your muscles in the gym, you can work out to build your brain function.

Every day, devote an allotted time, maybe 30 minutes or more, to a goal or problem. Write it down. Brainstorm ways to reach it or solve it. Keep reading, researching and thinking. If you can continue to do so for weeks and months, a switch will be turned on that you won't be able to shut off. Most of our minds are not truly working. Get your mind to working. We all underestimate our abilities. The only thing that is stopping us from reaching all our goals and dreams is our mind. How we think. Develop your mind and start functioning on a higher level than ever before.

A couple of years ago I could barely read five pages of a book a night. Consistently reading every day and night has raised that number over 10x. My mind is working and my problem-solving ability has grown. The best way to wake up an adult is to get them learning again. Get into learning by reading. Get the brain switched from "I can't" to the question, "How can I?" Now the mind starts to work.

Most people think that learning stops with high school or college; but really, education is a life-long pursuit. You are constantly learning, but the question is -- what sources are you getting your information from? It is very important to pick the right sources because ideas have consequences in your life. A self-directed education is so important. Being educated doesn't mean that you have to have sat in an institution of higher learning. Some of the greatest minds have not.

Being educated is not always signified by a certificate or diploma. I received a few in my life that were basically sheets of paper and only showed my completion of a program and not the knowledge of a subject. Harry Truman had no formal education and was considered one of the most educated presidents this country has had. It was because he read books every day. It wasn't Harry Potter or those romance novels. He developed a self-directed education.

Drink deeply from good books. Build your library of knowledge. Learn good principles to help develop your life. Apply those principles. Share them with others by passing along that information. Try to motivate those around you who are looking for something but don't quite know what they are looking for. Look through history and study all the great men and women who have accomplished great things. One thing that you will find that they all have in common is that they were all voracious readers! Try reading "The magic of thinking BIG" by David J. Schwartz, Ph.D. It puts a new spin on the way we think and why we think the way we do.

By now you have begun your shift. You have decided to take a higher path than perhaps many of your friends. Your actions are leading to better results because of the new information you have learned. You wanted to do better with your finances so you educated yourself on that subject by reading books by great financial authors like Dave Ramsey. You wanted to become a better leader and person of influence so you studied and associated with others who possess those qualities. Your marriage and personal relationships were not quite up to par so you listened to some audio CDs that helped propel those relationships forward.

Are you done? By no means! We must continue the process. We can never stop learning and growing. If you are not growing, you are dying. I'm not a grown man. Grown refers to the past tense. The graveyard is full of grown men. I am a growing man. We need to constantly be learning. Success is based in continually feeding your mind, body and spirit so that you can adapt to change and new information. Principles are forever. Facts can change. Continually learning keeps you in the game and focused on winning. Your work is not done and you have not arrived. You may have hit a good or even great point in your life, but you have further to go. There are not enough years left in your life for you to learn all that you need to learn. There is more available space in your brain than one could hardly imagine.

Your life should end with some unfinished work. Before you hit a goal, you should have set another one. No man, woman or child should be walking this earth without a goal that they aren't actively working on. If you stop learning and growing, the mind will begin the shut-down sequence. Staying on that path of a self-directed education means continually learning in order to continue the accumulation of better results and a better life. When you live a principle-centered life, the guarantee of the best life you can live is automatic.

A principle is a law that is established to create the environment to successfully produce the performance of what is promised. Every manufacturer builds into his products principles by which that product functions. If you follow those principles, everything that the manufacturer promised will happen. If you go against the principles of the design of that product, it will ultimately fail.

Success is based on following principles. Everything in life is built to function on principles. Principles are established to make life simple. If we can learn principles, we can simplify our lives. So many people are moving further away from the principles of life established from the beginning of time. This is why fewer and fewer people are finding and sustaining significant success in their life. God put systems into place so that everything will function as it should. When you don't know the principles, you go through trial and error, heartache and pain. Study the animal kingdom. They all follow the principles that God has established. They live off of instinct. Animals live successful lives as God intended. You don't have to teach a bird to fly south for the winter. He doesn't ask for directions and he doesn't pray to God for answers. He does what is already built inside of him. Animals will not function correctly if they eat the wrong foods. We are the same way. There are things that we were not made to consume and quantities of substances we consume that are contrary to the principles of our design.

Why do you think so many people are sick and develop deceases that they would not have if they followed the principles of dietary law? God wants us to function according to the principles established for us to be successful in all areas of life.

Success is not the material things we gain or possess. It is being or doing exactly what we were made to do. We must live our purpose. In order to find our purpose, we must follow God's principles and the answer to your purpose will appear. If you obey the principles, you can predict the outcome. When we keep following the wrong principles or follow no principle, that's when we get unpredictable results. Success evades us and we don't understand why. Don't look for the facts of life. They can change. Look for the eternal principles. Look for the truth and live by it. Read between the lines. Look for understanding of your purpose and live on purpose through the true principles of life.

CHAPTER 19

This Can Be the End or Your Beginning

"It is not the strongest of the species that survive, nor the most intelligent, but the one most responsive to change."

-Charles Darwin

The world doesn't care if you are a success or not. In the grand scheme of things, it doesn't matter if you get off of the path of average people and get on to the path of the Self-directed Shift or not. Your life will go on. You still live in the richest part of the world during the richest time in history. You will be fine. Life will go on. You will do everything that most people do on a daily basis. Your life will be lived, you will learn, and you will love. There may even be marginal success in different areas of your life.

Getting on the Self-directed Shift is intentionally seeking success and rising above others because you will do what they will not. You will live like no one else so that you can live like no one else. Your results will be greater than the average person because you will walk where average people are afraid of walking.

Your success in life is not determined by what happens to you but how you respond to those things that happen. My high school football coach said something many years ago that has stuck and resonates in my mind today. He said that we have to overcome adversity. The Self-directed shift is a path that pushes you over the huge boulder that falls at your feet. It gets you safely over the alligator-filled moat by providing you with the perfect drawbridge. You are not going to have a perfect life. It's going to get tough and at times it will seem as if you can't take all that is being thrown your way. Do not tuck your tail, ball yourself up in a knot, or run away and hide. What do you do? You have to do something! Some people give up and some people stand up. Many are knocked down in life and many of those people get up to fight again; but there are few who continuously get knocked down and refuse to stay down. They are on a Self-directed Shift. No matter how many times life puts you on the canvas, you have to get up, dust yourself off, and fight. I've watched people stay down and get counted out. I've watched others get out of the ring and watch others fight. I once found myself outside of those ropes scared to get back in, but knowing that my place in this world is standing toe to toe with every opponent that life brings my way. Life is not a spectator sport. I know that my place is contending for the heavyweight championship. My gloves are back on and my shoes have been laced. I am fighting because I know I can win. You can win. We all can win if we refuse to stay down. When you get up, study your opponent. Develop winning strategies. Find the right corner man and listen. Muhammad Ali knocked out George Foreman in a fight no one thought he could win. By all practicality at that point in Ali's life, he should not have lasted more than a few rounds, let alone KO the younger and stronger Foreman. He refused to be beat. He refused to give up.

What are you going to do today when life hits you from the blind side? Next week when you are hit square on the chin and your legs are cut from underneath you, what are you going to do? What about next month or next year? If you keep living and keep fighting, you're going to get hit. You're going to get knocked down. Get up and keep fighting. You are a champion. Overcome the adversities that life puts in front of you.

Early on, I thought I could save the world, or at least all of the people in my circle like family, friends and co-workers. I had information that could transform each one of our lives into the lives we all dreamed about and talked about. As I continue my own path, I realize that some don't want to step out of line. Are you ready to step out?

What I have is only information. Information alone will not solve your problems or help you succeed. You have to apply that information. It takes action and effort. Getting out of that line that you have been walking slowly, dragging your feet in, takes energy that so many are afraid to exert. I realized that although everyone has the ability to live extraordinary lives, only a few will. It's the Yin and the Yang. There is a certain balance in this world created by polar opposites. You can't have heroes without villains. The lion can't exist without the gazelle. There can be no old without the young. There are people in your life who will fill that space on the opposite end of the spectrum from where you stand, and you must be okay with that.

As frustrating as it may be, you can't force them into seeing what you see or doing what you do. I can't force you into applying the information and principles that you have read in this book. Everyone must embrace the shift themselves and start the journey only when they are ready. Sadly, there are many who will live their entire life without getting out of that line. It doesn't matter how much information you put before them. It doesn't matter that they know the truth and see the correct path. They choose not to get out of line.

Most of us don't need more information. We know what foods we should be eating; we know we should be exercising; we know we shouldn't be in a relationship with this person; we know we should be saving and investing money, and educating ourselves. We don't because it takes action and effort.

On your journey, let those go who don't want to follow the path of excellence. Expending all of your energy towards those who are stuck in the mud will only slow you down and knock you off your track. Help those who want to be helped. I have no problem with turning around to come get you as long as you don't pull in the opposite direction. We all must realize when it is time to let go and let God save them. You have a duty to yourself to be the best and most successful person you can be in this life. I'm sorry mama, daddy, brother, sister, friend, son or daughter. I'm on a Self-directed Shift!

I'm looking for freedom. My journey on the path of a Self-directed shift is a journey for freedom. During my whole life I have felt imprisoned; not the self-imposed prison I talked about earlier. One that seemed forced by outside sources. Looking back and looking at the path I was once on, I realize that I was indeed incarcerated. I even saw the look on others' faces that indicated that they too were not free. We were slaves. Many are still slaves to this day. Some of my own family members and close friends are locked up without a clue as to how to get themselves out. They won't even let me post bail for them. The sadder fact is that the jail cell that they are imprisoned in is very much like the jail in the small town of Mayberry, policed by Andy Griffin and Barney Fife. You too may be in that cell. All you have to do is reach your arms through the bars, grab the keys, and unlock the gate.

We just don't realize that the key is just in our reach. I'm reaching for those keys as Barney sleeps. One may not be free and not realize it. Knowledge creates freedom. Wealth creates freedom. We are often in an illusion that we are free. If you are free, leave your home today and go to Paris, Jamaica or some distant place you have dreamed of traveling to. Without money you are not free to do the things you want or need. In many cases, without money you can't live. If you needed life-saving surgery that costs $150k would you be able to pay for your life? Some people can and some cannot. Do you have a choice? Think about your life. How many choices do you have? That is freedom. How free are you? I know people who are truly free. How many months can you survive? Are you free? When will you be free?

What hurt me some time ago was when I realized that there are people in this world who are no better than I, no smarter, no more talented or no more deserving than me and my family, but they enjoy a life of freedom that has alluded us for quite some time. How is it that Santa couldn't bring me that special toy when Timmy who lived right next door got it? His parents had a little more freedom. Can you stop working? Does it feel impossible to enjoy your life because you are in a rat race with a hundred others and there's just one piece of cheese? Realize that you're not free and find a way out. If Mayberry's town drunk, Otis, can free himself, so can you. Remember this. He put his own self in that cell.

The human mind is so remarkable. It can produce the life you want to live. We just need to help it develop so that it can spring forth an abundant life of our choosing in any and all areas we desire. Successful people tap into the vast resources of their mind, their thoughts and the actions that only come from the right thinking. Why are there so many people not living the successful lives that they can be living? They just don't understand what is so obvious to a select few of the people walking this earth. Thoughts become things. Our thinking builds upon our belief systems. Our beliefs force us to act in a way that is different from average people so that we can achieve the results that go beyond those results that average people acquire. If you don't have the right mindset and thinking process you have to change. You can change. It takes work to train the mind especially when your paradigm has been the same way for so many years. It will just take a little amount of work for it to happen.

Start small. Do little things to create a shift in your thinking. Read good books that have already changed the lives of millions of people. It doesn't matter who you are. It doesn't matter where you are in your life. Your past does not have to dictate your future. You can be the person you want to be. You can have all that you wish and dream of. Your success will come if you start a Self-directed Shift.

Start with one particular area of your life that you may want or need to make a change in. Understand and know that that change is possible. Focus on learning everything you can about that subject. Read books that deal in that particular subject matter, find magazines and news articles about it, look for videos and blogs tackling the same issue, and seek wise counsel from people who are well versed in the area you need to make a change in. You have to do it. It is imperative that you start right now with some type of movement forward. Take the small steps that others are not willing to take. Be consistent and take those steps often. You may not see the change right away, but you will see the change eventually. You will project yourself off of the path of average people to a path that only a few take. You are on a Self-directed Shift.

Ball Game.

Mr. Rickey Lewis has given us a blueprint and guide to an intelligent refusal to be overwhelmed by the stress epidemic surrounding us. He presents practical guidance to help us deal with overload. His advance is indispensable for health and sanity today and opens the way for serious discipline and personal growth in LIFE.

Sam A. Khani

Success Entrepreneur and Life Coach

Rickey Lewis is more than an inspiration. He has taken his own experiences and developed life lessons that cover every topic such as happiness, success, finances, relationships, leadership, discipline and so much more. It has the key to make immediate and profound changes in any or every area of your life! If you want to maximize your greatest potential, this book will be all you need to guide you with your Self-directed Shift.

Jamie Dominguez

Staff Sergeant-United States Air Force

BSN-RN Student

The Self-directed Shift is the name Rickey Lewis, one of my mentors, my motivators, and most importantly one of my best friends, has decided to name this book. It has been a lifelong story of his. I have seen the growth of this man and it has truly been amazing. He has definitely been on a self-directed shift at the same time helping so man others to also be on the same transformation that he is on. Please I encourage everyone to read and understand this book. Share this book with someone you care about. I was taught that if you want to do something in life, find someone who has already done it and do like them. I can honestly say, Rickey Lewis has done the work and just happened to be around for the ride. I made some mistakes that took me down a road I wasn't trying to travel. Rickey was right there to encourage me to pick myself up. He helped me realize that I was better than that and that my best was yet to come. I instantly started learning success principle from him and was able to turn what could have been a dead-end life into a life of accomplishment and my on little successes. Even though I'm still traveling the roads of life my journey is great and continually getting better. I give much credit to Rickey Lewis for being there and helping me start my own Self-directed Shift.

Lonnie Bradley II,

Business Owner

Jindal Tubular-Logistics Supervisor

Real Estate Investor

Community Organization President

Former Property of the United States Federal Prison System

Mandy Cuevas thank you Rickey Lewis; I needed to read this first thing this morning. I will desperately need some guidance regarding "forgiveness"
Like · Reply · 6y

Lucretia Lott Well put, and very inspiring and so totally on point with what just happened these last few days. Thanks Rickey Lewis perfect timing!
Like · Reply · 6y

Chiara Ishem Smith Amen!! I was laughing and crying all at the same time (tears of joy)! Thanks for those memories....you definitely made my day!!
Like · Reply · 6y

JW Boothe Thank you Big Brother for being a Guardian Angel and supporting Final Salute! I hope enough people help in time to save our home!
Like · Reply · 6y

Shenea Kissy Bell Loved this post as well!! Citronella and I talked about your Positive, Encouraging post last week!! They are helpful and encouraging...keep them coming!!! I Love the analogy of life and the building that you use!!!...you should put that on a poster!!! Perhaps you should put these posts in a book and publish it!!!;it's really that good!!!!
Like · Reply · 6y

Mary Day I am soo proud of U.working with youth. May God bless and keep in his spirit.
Like · Reply · 6y

Carl Shoemaker wow, coach. This is amazing. I know ive felt exactly like what u were describing there
Like · Reply · 7y

Sonyetta Harris Words of wisdom. Very well said Ricky! Keep the post coming! Love the positive vibes I get when I read them!
Like · Reply · 7y

Kelly Galloway All I want is change! Well said Rickey!
Like · Reply · 7y

Thomas Snyder This is the best stuff i have read in a while. Keep it up coach I really enjoy reading your daily inspirations!
Like · Reply · 7y

Shenea Kissy Bell Another GREAT message!!! Love it!!! Keep them coming!!
Oh!! and Mrs Tate was a GREAT teacher.....I had her too!!! Ive always remembered her enthusiasm on a daily basis....even as a young child!!! It's one thing I've kept in mind as I teach daily!!! You could tell she loved it; therefore, she was GREAT!!!!
Like · Reply · 7y

Rachel Price i believe....this one was outstanding. Kinda like hearing the Val at graduation. Great speech Ricky.
Like · Reply · 7y

Marvin Singleton reading your messages everyday give me something to look forward to. First thing I do in the morning is thank God for letting me see another day and then I read your messages.your message have true meaning behind them. May your day be Bless.
Like · Reply · 7y

Marcus N Tammy Cuevas Keep up the great words of wisdom ...we enjoy your post have a great day
Like · Reply · 7y

Tenicka Strown Hi Rickey, first of all I am proud of you ; more importantly, god is proud. I am not really on facebook that much , as my love language is quality time, so face to face works better for me. Having said that, when I do check in and read messages like yours, leaves me overwhelmed with joy, it is inspiring to see how gods work is beng fulfilled in your life andhow he uses you as his vessel. Thank you for uplifting my spirits this morning, may god continue to bless you an your beautiful family. Tenicka....
Like · Reply · 7y

DeVaughn Rodney Jiles Thanks for sharing Rickey Lew.... Your msgs are always appreciated.
Like · Reply · 7y

Rita Regina Davis That's so true. Once a person takes responsibility for their own actions. Everything else will fall into place. God Bless you
Like · Reply · 7y

Lillian Marie Lizana-Cooper Man, Rickey, this message MUST be spread. Let me do my part...Please let me print this out and tape it up at work this weekend, for starters. Because you have Truly inspired me. True Wisdom, True. Thank you for sharing! 😊
Like · Reply · 7y

Larry McFadden It was no accident that we met in Gulfport. My dream is to follow the plan that God has for me as a street evangelist, and meet people's needs as the Lord shows me things. Satan would like to remind me of my failures, but God says that in his book, there is no record of failure. God bless you.
Like · Reply · 6y

Charles E. Joseph There's a book here!
Like · Reply · 7y

Reggie StReggie Williams Man I had the same conversation just yesterday.... This is the gospel...what's ya number Ricky?
Like · Reply · 7y

Jana DeDeaux That's powerful stuff Ricky. Thanks for the reassurance that there are still soldiers fighting for the truth. Its not loosing battle.
Like · Reply · 7y

Shenea Kissy Bell Good!!! You certainly can do it!!! I truly look forward to your post!!!
I've always wanted to write a book also....I think I may once I retire!!
Like · Reply · 7y

Shenea Kissy Bell Again, I say Outstanding!!!! If you take your posts and staple them together, I will buy them!!!!
You are TRULY on to something real big here!!!! I see Best Selling books (plural) and Major Seminars (plural) in your future!!!!!!!!!
Like · Reply · 7y

Deven Sharron Some people look forward to reading the daily paper...me I look forward to reading my cousin's daily messages...God places things on your heart and mind that are truly a blessing to those who take the time to not only read, but understand as well. Thank you!
Like · Reply · 7y

Mission Cook Good point Coach!! We have to speak life into our children's life. Believe in their dreams and motivate them to follow their dreams. There is so much power in the words we speak, so speak life. I SPEAK LIFE......

Alexander Jacobs That one hit home right about now. I do just that same thing when times get hard. I talk to myself "suck it up ,I got this".The Lord has never failed me .It is said he will never give you more than you can handle.i always know that things can be so much worse.I give thanks for the good times and even the bad.
Like · Reply · 7y

Tiffany Jones Wow well said; this is another great book that I must read. Knowing just from the few words you've spoken. Amazing! U inspire me...
Like · Reply · 7y

Lena Dailey Surely did need this today cause the kids that I work with always want to know something if not everything
Like · Reply · 7y

Danwaile Karpinski Very Nicely put Mr. Lewis. I can truly relate to this message...we all have alot of negativity that surrounds us each day, and yes it is up to us to as to which direction we will let it lead us. Great One. Glad you got through your day in one piece.
Like · Reply · 7y

Ari'el Wilkerson im so proud of u cuz. thanks, cuz u hav no idea that God was jus dealing w/me on that yesterday. love ya much
Like · Reply · 7y

Haley McCandless lol. I often try to hit share and I can't do it. I have even tried copy and pasted your stuff and I still can't figure out how to do it since it's lengthy. If you know how---- let me know. A lot of ppl I care about could really benefit from the things you write about.
Like · Reply · 7y

Iris Lizana-y Thanks Rickey really needed to hear/see some thing encouraging and you always seem to know how to lift the spirits of others. Just so you know I see and appreciate the posts.
Like · Reply · 7y

Tanesha Harvey Darensbourg I love this Rickey, I have been without a job for a entire year. During the time I was employed, I ended up just like we all do paycheck to paycheck, above my means. When I lost my job, reality set in, so I really had to look at my finances! I have changed my attitude towards my spending habits, and even now that im not working I am doing better financially! All by making those small and sometimes big sacrifices we need to make in order to become debt free oneday. I am not there yet, but im on my way. 6 months worth of savings is what society says we need just in case you loose your job. I didn't have quite as much, but God has provided for me, and added to my account! Can I get a amen!
Like · Reply · 7y

Shellon Lawton Walker "information rich & wisdom poor" ... great one, jotting that down for later
Like · Reply · 7y

Tracy Anne Joseph Ding ding ding! Nail on the head. Read and then think about what you've read. Process it...just like the body has to process the foods we eat, our minds need to process the words we read. Otherwise, it's all for naught. AMEN!
Like · Reply · 7y

Fred Hall Lol! It wasnt a day of high school that you didnt have me laughing and even @ practice . Kml at pig joke I needed that laugh!
Like · Reply · 7y

Tranesa Shanell Bradley Wow!! This is True Inspiration!! I love it! I will have to take some time to change my normals and read this book! Sounds like I will be in for a great journey as I read it!
Like · Reply · 7y

BK Livestrong Great words Rickey Lewis! I needed to read this to start my day! God Bless you brother.
Like · Reply · 7y

Susan Abbott Thank you for being so you! Uncle Frank is up in heaven with a big, cheesy grin on, knowing you are a fine man!
Like · Reply · 7y

Deneene Bell Zayzay Great stuff Rickey, Just like waking up on the wrong side of the bed happens ,staying there is a choice -'Tomiko Fraser "
Like · Reply · 7y

Yolanda Christophe
May 7 at 8:34 AM

Rickey Lewis You Are Amazing!! Thanks For All You Do For Our Kiddos 💜💜

Latasha Robinson Gyins Those kids love you, so thank you for being awesome I'm so many young people's lives.
Like · Reply · 1w

Terri Webb Thank you for being such a good mentor for our kids! We appreciate you
Love · Reply · 1w

Chance Edler Don't sell yourself short Coach, you're a real teacher and a very good one at that.
Love · Reply · 1w

Jeremy Martin Thanks Ricky, thanks for supporting my restaurant, at times I feel complacent because I'm a business owner but then I shake it off because I want a bigger place and want my product in every store Possible, these words you spoke made my mind tick harder ... thanks big homie
Love · Reply · 3w

Dee Fairley
May 4 at 10:17 AM

Good Advice Rickey Lewis... Lord help me to sharpen my Axe!
Show Attachment

You, Felisha Peachez Crawford and 1 other

Kelly Galloway As always well said. Everyday I wake up I think about encouraging words, and I no I could always depend on u and Jason to give them to me. Thanks! Love yall
Like · Reply · 7y

Chris Patten Any author that can incoporate a milli vanilli into the moral is ok by me. Well said!!!!
Like · Reply · 7y

LaMar Raboteau Man, I was just hosting a pity party. Thanks for ruining my party. I needed that for real.
Like · Reply · 7y

Perry Williams If I am what I read then I am gonna turn into Uncle Bama.....because I am reading the book called "The Life of Rickey Lewis", on the slick side.
like · Reply · 7y

Windy West Stanton Very well spoken Rickey. I have friends who are very hurt by the slander of others. Friendships have been broken over this election. I hope you don't mind, but I am reposting your post. Thanks for your leadership in our community. :)
Like · Reply · 7y

Nicole Morgan Jones Boy.......did your write that?????? You better go:) Awesome
Like · Reply · 7y

Deneene Bell Zayzay Well said and I have seen this take place in the last few month's ,weeks and days leading up to last nights election.Great friendships gone over difference's in political views. Just like you said,some things we must learn to keep to self. We should be moving forward and not looking back . I also had to re-post and I hope someone in my circle of friends will re-post and everyone can get the chance to read your post (a must read) Thanks.
ke · Reply · 7y

Sam Khani I missed hanging out with you . I learn something every time .
Like · Reply · 7y

Lori O. Hinds Good words Rick Lewis!!! You are absolutely right. I have told my youngest son that I became a crutch to him. I know that it is never too late! He is going to get hungry once again!
Like · Reply · 3w

Sonya Dedeaux
April 22 at 11:19 AM

Finally,,,back running 3 miles,,,and not too shabby on the time either,,,had a lil encouragement from COACH Lewis (Rickey) last night and got it done. Ok I'm done for the week lol,,,not really,,,let's see how long I can keep this up
#runninggoals #3milesin3weeks

Richard Torres So of the brightest insight I heard all year
Love · Reply · 2d

Cory Watts My wife and I had a similar discussion about our kids. What we discussed and discovered is that our lack of and our impoverished situation pushed us to want more. We defined that push as hunger. We must discover what pushes or kids and/or create their hunger by removing comforts.
Like · Reply · 2w

Mary Robinson Tinsley Sharpening my blade with LOTS of Personal Growth and Development 🔪❤️‼️
Love · Reply · 1w

C Mac Labat Dude................. Keep speaking life some of us need it! 🙏🏽❤️
Like · Reply · 3w

Linda Watkins Savage You said a mouth full and all I can say is Amen. May your hunger continue. Bless you Rickey..much love.

Love · Reply · 3w · ♡ 1

Sonya Bowser Ashley Thank you for your motivation Rickey Lewis! Don't grow weary in well doing. You are appreciated!

Like · Reply · 3w · Edited · ♡♡ 2

Jay Lanning Rickey Lewis you continue to post these Videos it helps so many you just dont know. Im an old soul and some of the inspections you have shared have made me look in the mirror. All i know i am blessed to call you a Brother.

Like · Reply · 3w · ♡♡ 4

Carlos Malley Rickey, I don't chime in much, but NEVER stop pushing these inspirational messages out to the world. You are an exceptional leader and I appreciate you keeping me (us) in the loop of what God places on your heart to share with the world and inspire each of us to be better. Salute teammate and friend!

Love · Reply · 3w · ♡ 3

Arlean Porche You are absolutely right, we should strive to be our very best. Stay hungry Mr. Rickey Lewis so that you can continue to enlighten others to be an inspiration and to reach out and share their wisdom and life lessons with others. Be blessed. Great message.

Curtis Cotten Jr. great message coach... you gave me my copy of the book... 8 years ago... I still live by the principle... great message.

Love · Reply · 3w · ♡ 1

Jay Lanning Amazing talk man never looked at it like that....... I tell you what after this 10 percent will go away....

Like · Reply · 7w · ♡ 1

Paige Necaise Cobb This is one of your best ones!

Love · Reply · 8w · ♡ 1

Scottie Cuevas Coach I really enjoy reading your post and meal plans. Thanks for sharing.

Like · Reply · 8w · ♡ 1

Melissa Malley Williams Good message! It is all about the mindset. Love that effort must rise above excuses. You will find the sweet spot when your passion collides with your strengths. Preach!

Love · Reply · 8w · ♡♡ 2

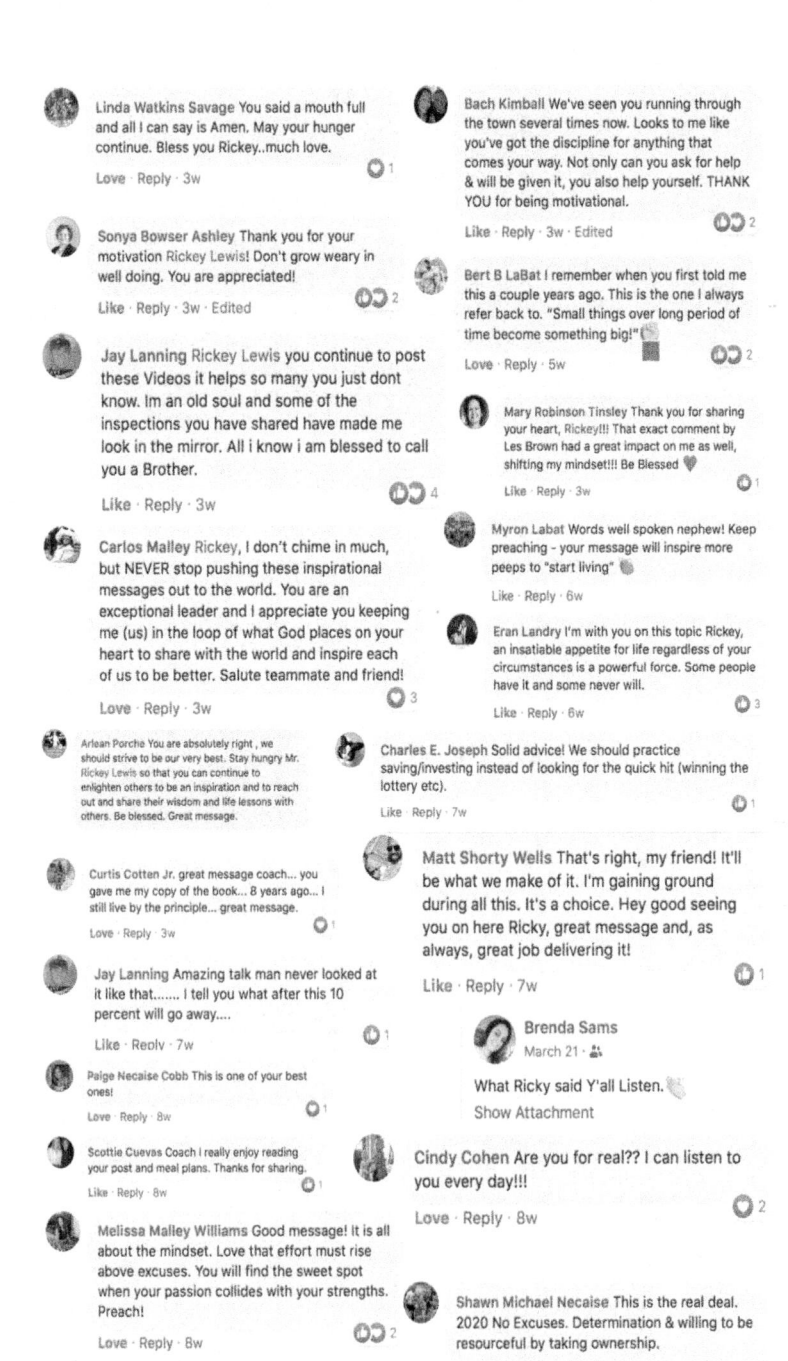

Angelia Michelle Wallace Let Him use you Rickey Lewis! You are helping some folks!

Love · Reply · 8w · ♡ 1

Bach Kimball We've seen you running through the town several times now. Looks to me like you've got the discipline for anything that comes your way. Not only can you ask for help & will be given it, you also help yourself. THANK YOU for being motivational.

Like · Reply · 3w · Edited · ♡♡ 2

Bert B LaBat I remember when you first told me this a couple years ago. This is the one I always refer back to. "Small things over long period of time become something big!"

Love · Reply · 5w · ♡♡ 2

Mary Robinson Tinsley Thank you for sharing your heart, Rickey!!! That exact comment by Les Brown had a great impact on me as well, shifting my mindset!!! Be Blessed 💜

Like · Reply · 3w · ♡ 1

Myron Labat Words well spoken nephew! Keep preaching - your message will inspire more peeps to "start living"

Like · Reply · 6w

Eran Landry I'm with you on this topic Rickey, an insatiable appetite for life regardless of your circumstances is a powerful force. Some people have it and some never will.

Like · Reply · 6w · ♡ 3

Charles E. Joseph Solid advice! We should practice saving/investing instead of looking for the quick hit (winning the lottery etc).

Love · Reply · 7w · ♡ 1

Matt Shorty Wells That's right, my friend! It'll be what we make of it. I'm gaining ground during all this. It's a choice. Hey good seeing you on here Ricky, great message and, as always, great job delivering it!

Like · Reply · 7w · ♡ 1

Brenda Sams
March 21 ·

What Ricky said Y'all Listen.
Show Attachment

Cindy Cohen Are you for real?? I can listen to you every day!!!

Love · Reply · 8w · ♡ 2

Shawn Michael Necaise This is the real deal. 2020 No Excuses. Determination & willing to be resourceful by taking ownership.

You're going somewhere BIG Rickey, but you gotta believe it first! I believe in you big time!

Love · Reply · 8w · ♡ 2

Tram Nguyen Great video Coach!! Keep sharing your motivating ideas to the world! 👍

Like · Reply · 10w

Bradley Lonnie Great one Rickey Lord knows I usually say man I wish this or I wish that but wishes and dreams are just that till action is applied. Also, because of my naturally competitive nature I love being around so many positive people like yourself, Leo Hawkins and so so many more people who push me to continue to drive forward and don't settle for anything but greatness. Sometimes it gets rough for all of us but when you got a Great team the Super Bowl is easy to win.

Love · Reply · 8w

Paula Henderson Thanks cousin in law, I needed this motivation speech. I'll be back on my work out tomorrow strong.

Like · Reply · 10w

Tammie DeDeaux Gray I love more than anything, the fact you and your boys are running together!! Spending quality time together!

Love · Reply · 16w

Derrick Willis 😄 "Do you really love yourself if you're not disciplined "?

Like · Reply · 29w

Perry Williams
September 17, 2019 · 🌎

We must overcome False Evidence Appearing Real!!!
#SuccessBuildingPrinciples
Show Attachment

Betty Mechatto Thank you for your awesome words!! Yes, we all need to hear this!! Praise GOD 🙏 ❤

Like · Reply · 35w

Vanessa Roberts You give me Joy, just by listening to your message. Love you son.

Love · Reply · 37w

Merle Josephine I wish there were MORE MEN in the world like you Rickey Lewis! 👏👏 You are truly amazing. Keep sharing and spreading knowledge to the youth. ❤

Love · Reply · 38w

Jay Lanning Children learn what they live. You are an inspiration and a role model to many. As your wife is. Stay Strong i will share this as i am a father of 5 Amazing Boys myself.

Like · Reply · 38w

Natalia A. Davis Wow Rickey! Talk about acceptance of accountability, and responsibility! I really enjoy listening to your heartfelt, honest, and candid conversations. I am so glad that you share them with us, because I for one find them inspiring, and motivational. Sometimes life hands us situations daily, and each individual situation evokes various emotions/responses from us.

Like · Reply · 7w

Debra Carter Most definitely thank you for your speech I so needed to hear this also 😌

Like · Reply · 13w

Destiny Pierce Thank you for always sharing your words of wisdom which seems to always be at such a needed time. ❤

Love · Reply · 13w

Dee Virdell Yes, incentives are great motivation tools ‼ awesome dad keep being a great life coach your sons are learning from you.

Love · Reply · 15w · Edited

Carol Grubbs Santiago So thankful 🙌 you are a great role model for your sons. They are blessed ❤

Love · Reply · 16w

Ursula Oustalet Meaux I needed to hear this today... thank you for the blessing you are sharing with us! 🙏

Like · Reply · 22w

Marcus Whitfield
September 17, 2019 · 🌎
Do the things in which you FEAR... and the DEATH of FEAR in certain!!! Great word Rickey Lewis
Show Attachment
👍❤ Rebeca Gonzalez Berker and 3 others

Allyson Hardenburgh Williams You restore my hope with your posts. ❤ you my friend!

Love · Reply · 35w

Lisa Truong Life is too short and shorter by the day. My dad use to tell me one door close another door open .

Like · Reply · 37w

Stephen Jordan Well said Rickey Lewis, I have a ton of yards to cut and it's too wet but this joy in my heart and spirit is well and alive. Great message brother!

Like · Reply · 37w

Lorraine Walker And lately I honestly been thinking about this.I went to school for this reason you saying right here and i some how just paused.I am so unhappy at times with my job now.You just said something my inner self was saying.Now it's time to make a move

Like · Reply · 41w

Shekhinah Yisra'el Someone really needed to hear this ..this morning. Awesome message. I also appreciate the praise you give your wife.. as all men should. Thanks.

Like · Reply · 38w

Golden Ann Fairconnetue Rickey Father T was a all around guy he came from good stock. You and a few other young men came along at the right time and the right place! So thank you for the encouraging words.

Like · Reply · 43w

Bradley Lonnie Well said Rickey supporting the small businesses will open up opportunities for other people in your community and open up minds and hearts of those same people great job Bama keep pushing

Like · Reply · 49w

Shaun Piernas I tell all the youngsters around me the same things bruh. Keep pushing your message, you were built for this man!!!

Love · Reply · 51w

Rhonda Ladner Rickey Lewis it was an honor having you teach all my kids!! Thank you for being such an inspiration to them!! I love watching all your speeches!!! Keep them coming!!

Love · Reply · 51w

William Shaw Positive thoughts create positive reality...even in the midst of adversity, challenging times, etc. We are masters of our own reality and our approach and mentality towards living is up to us. Thanks for the insightful message coach. Be your best self!

Like · Reply · 1y

Jakia Kiki Williams Good video. I remember I was happy you were my friend when I was in Illinois people would cut out news article and brag like they knew you. Valley Love

Like · Reply · 1y

Brenda M Varnado So true Rickey Lewis. The bridges you burn and the words you speak. Bridges burnt most likely we may desire to cross again, however they're gone, and be careful of the words, ugly words don't taste so good when you have to eat them. Keep up the good work Rick.

Like · Reply · 1y

Aaron Farve I still remember that speech u gave me in high school.... Thank u....

Like · Reply · 1y

Lisa Raymond GREAT MESSAGE..TEACH 1,REACH 1..THAT'S WHAT GOD SAYS.

Like · Reply · 2y

Launa Murray ...and "trying" is failing with flying colors. When my kids say "I'll try" I always tell them they are checking out on me— you either do it or you don't. There's no "Trying." When you say you are "trying," you are giving yourself an excuse to fail!

Like · Reply · 51w

Billy Dedeaux Amen..anything is possible if you put ur mind to work..Thanks Rickey Lewis

Like · Reply · 48w · Edited

Tommy Searight Jr. How can I? Self-Awareness is everything!

Like · Reply · 48w

Alvie Shepherd Being intentional is exactly what it takes to accomplish goals etc.. Great post brother! #YESYOUCAN

Like · Reply · 48w

La'Sha Parker Awesome 👏 this needed to be said!!! There is a group of young guys that I reach out to also. I have a few of them on Snapchat and they definitely needs to hear this!!!

Like · Reply · 1y

Treasa Welborn Rickey Lewis you are always right on time....thank you for the words! Hugs and love!

Barbara Mayfield This is so true, always take your time and think. When I was a teacher, my instruction to my Special Education students was count to 10. This will give you time to think before you speak.

Like · Reply · 1y

Hanslizae Cook Good point Rickey, it seems like you hit on subjects I'm involved with 😊. There's a saying my grandfather told me that I live by still today, he said " baby always be nice to people and help people because you never know when your entertaining angels 👼. Recently I was able to save someone from a major obstacle that could have impacted there life and this same person wasn't appreciative everyone around them was they actually did some mean things to me afterwards I pulled my plug and decided to just let them be. A friend of mine told me your heart is too big I said I guarantee they will regret me leaving them than the other way around.

Elizabeth Ozene This was uplifting & very much needed Thanks!!!

Like · Reply · 1y

Diane Saucier U a good person may God keep blessing u and ur family I love you cause u is a very very good person

Love · Reply · 2y

Jacqueline Spaulding No magic!! Its law! Law of attraction...you manifest your reality with your thoughts...you feel it, you meditate (pray) on it, envision it, work towards it, your energy you put into it is heard by the universe and returns it to you ....you are connected to the universe and it is here to give u what u put out...just like a boomerang..u throw it out, it comes back ...power of the mind is not a joke (like Drake says in the song Both) #facts #lawofattraction #manifestyourreality #youareincontrol #positievibesonly

Like · Reply · 2y

Citronella Davis "Success leaves clues!" I love that.

Like · Reply · 3y

Travon Payne We are all practically family truth be told...learn your past, your people and their struggles to enhance your future...leave that negative mentality behind and find a way to produce positively! #Bayway...Union Washington and oh yeah Easterbrook!

Like · Reply · 3y

Darlene L. Lee Yes, Truly blessed because there's someone else who's worse off than you, someone else who'd love to be in your shoes

Nicole Thornton Just keep being yourself. Trust me, it's more than enough. Blessings to you.

Like · Reply · 1y

Sharron Henry I so needed to hear that Mr.rickey 🙏🏽💯🙌🏽... sometime we need to just breath for a moment 🙏

Like · Reply · 1y · Edited

Janita Cole Thank you cousin. Feels good to just breathe for a moment. Aaahhhhh

Like · Reply · 1y

Zachery Seth Williams You need to start publishing this stuff coach! Very true and inspiring words!

Like · Reply · 7y

Shenea Kissy Bell Again, I say Outstanding!!!! If you take your posts and staple them together, I will buy them!!!! You are TRULY on to something real big here!!! I see Best Selling books (plural) and Major Seminars (plural) in your future!!!!!!!!!

Like · Reply · 7y

Carlos Malley Rickey, I'm humbled brother and honored to make this list. To God be the glory for my only goal is too decrease, so He may increase. Praying for you and yours......Los

Like · Reply · 7y

Francois Lewis Amen, well spoken, moving, inspiring and motivating! Beautiful and uplifting message! Thanks, my brother! God bless!

Like · Reply · 42w

Johnny Lott
June 18, 2018

My boy Rickey Lewis speaking and telling real facts please listen 🎯💯
👏🏽💯🙌🏽
Show Attachment

Kendrick Laneaux Man, I love Bama!!!! Bra, i swear to God you dont understand how good i feel after listening to you just telling the damn truth!! Love ya playa... BACK-A-TOWN, USA BAB!!!!! STAND UP!!!

Like · Reply · 3y

Travis Crawford Perfectly said... you always had a gift of words and I was glad I had the honor of playing ball with you.. you have come a long way and are a great role model for the community and I salute ya Rickey Lewis

Like · Reply · 3y

Jevon Vontoure Well said Rickey. In your tool box you'll find me, I am to be used, to aid in the journey of progress however and by whoever so just keep me polished and maintained so that I may work to your favor effectively.
#elainesLounge #bridgebuilder

Kenneth Dedeaux Well put Rickey couldn't agree wit you more, you are a positive influence proud to be a friend

Like · Reply · 3y

Barbara Mayfield Great topic, when you truly love God and yourself from within, you do not care about people who likes you. When you see them, smile and pray for them but keep moving.

Like · Reply · 1y

Dale Peoples Blessed to have gotten the chance to play aside you on the football field, you were a leader then and still a leader now. Congrats Mr. Lewis

Love · Reply · 1y

LaMar Raboteau Thanks for the motivation, Rick. Your words seem to always be right on time. May God continue to use you as a vessel. Like Tracy said, stay fired up!

Like · Reply · 7y

Jeanne Alexander I would have just marked like but I loved it and thank you for being a great mentor to our youth

Like · Reply · 7y

Tracy Anne Joseph Amen, Rickey! It's wonderful to see that you get it and are so eagerly sharing with all of us. This is exciting. i look forward to your status updates. My hope is that some us sleeping out here will wake up and get it too. We must be purposeful in all that we do! Thank you, again, for sharing. And just to let you know, I'm a note taker...just saying...

Like · Reply · 7y

Gregory Newell I appreciate all them views, but its nice to see My first cousin seed Ricky Lewis do extraordinary things.

Like · Reply · 15w

Key'a Saucier The way to predict the future is to create it they say you change the mind you change the man mindset is key

Like · Reply · 41w

Kendrick Laneaux How it's like you always talking to me bra!!! You dont even have to say " Good morning afternoon or night" and just say "Look Popa this is what you need to do"!!! Lol.. Thanks Bama!! You my dude..

Love · Reply · 1y

Connie Gomillion Your right this just inspired me and I'm sure it did others also.

Like · Reply · 1y

Lisa Marie Bradley You did great at the funeral hope and wish you touched most hopefully all those kids 🙏🙏

Love · Reply · 1y

Treasa Welborn Rickey Lewis this is just how I am feeling this morning....I am tired of giving advice and its time they get off their own nails and do for themselves

Love · Reply · 1y

Cornelia Jennings Man, I was craving and wanting a peanut butter and jelly sandwich for the last week, I took this post differently! Lol

Like · Reply · 1y

Romelles N Erin Wilkerson What you do is amazing, you bring wisdom to the young people you come in contact with everyday and some adults who will take the advice, I take a leadership class every year to continue to teach me how to deal with people as I'm in a supervisor role at my company and it's taught me a great deal about not just leading the team I have, but also respecting the different personalities that we come in contact with everyday. If we had more people like you the next generation would know how to listen and learn from the people we come in contact with everyday, keep doing what you do and I enjoy your videos, God bless you and your family.

Like · Reply · 1y

Barbara Mayfield Great topic, when you truly love God and yourself from within, you do not care about people who likes you. When you see them, smile and pray for them but keep moving.

Like · Reply · 1y

Golden Ann Fairconnetue Mama always said people who don't care about you forget your name the day after you are buried! So ur right focus on people who love you!

Like · Reply · 1y

Precious Wallace Great message Rickey..... Me personally I take 200 pics and I'll post 198 of em lol.... #imconceited kmi....(my daddy told me I was pretty too many times)....... I love how God made me and the reflection I see when I look in the mirror..... If I look fat or have a double chin and I don't like it, maybe I should look at what's on the plate in front of me and do something to change what I don't like if that be the case....

Love · Reply · 2y

Mona Graham Great advice I think we all need to hear this at some point in our lives.

Like · Reply · 1y

Tiffany Hansbury-Davis Facts! You definitely need people to buy into you. You can change the product, but YOU are your brand!

Like · Reply · 1y

Arlean Porche Good morning Mr. Rickey Lewis, thank you for those encouraging words. I am ready to get off that nail and make some changes in my life. Praise God for greatness.

Love · Reply · 1y

Marcus Whitfield Boy this one here 👏👏👏

You can either go through the pain of change and start to make it better... or the pain of regret

Like · Reply · 1y

LpLike Paul Say EVERYTHING you said in this video, one more time, for the people in the back...... they didnt hear you!!! 📢📢📢

Like · Reply · 1y

Al Williamson I've sett in my car before work an watched your video 3 times. I needed that this morning. Was going in an tell my supervisor I don't feel good. After watching video I'm going in a roll the wheels of this truck cause the goal is to get the 💰💼

Love · Reply · 1y

Denise Dedeaux Barnett Going through some things right now and you have encouraged me to keep pushing. Thank you!

Love · Reply · 1y

Brenda M Varnado U do whats right at all times to the best of your ability. U are absolutely right! Everyone is not gonna like you. Lose, no sleep over it. Please God, that's the ultimate goal. Amen and Amen you don't need a cosigner for this message.

Like · Reply · 1y

Brian Pearse Wonderful message we are fearfully and wonderfully made. What I hear a lot of is I gotta loose 10 pounds. Then I'll be photographed a year later I hear the same song and the beauty of the person is still there

Like · Reply · 2y

Desiree Scandurro So thankful that you're my sons coach 🙏🙏🙏

Like · Reply · 2y

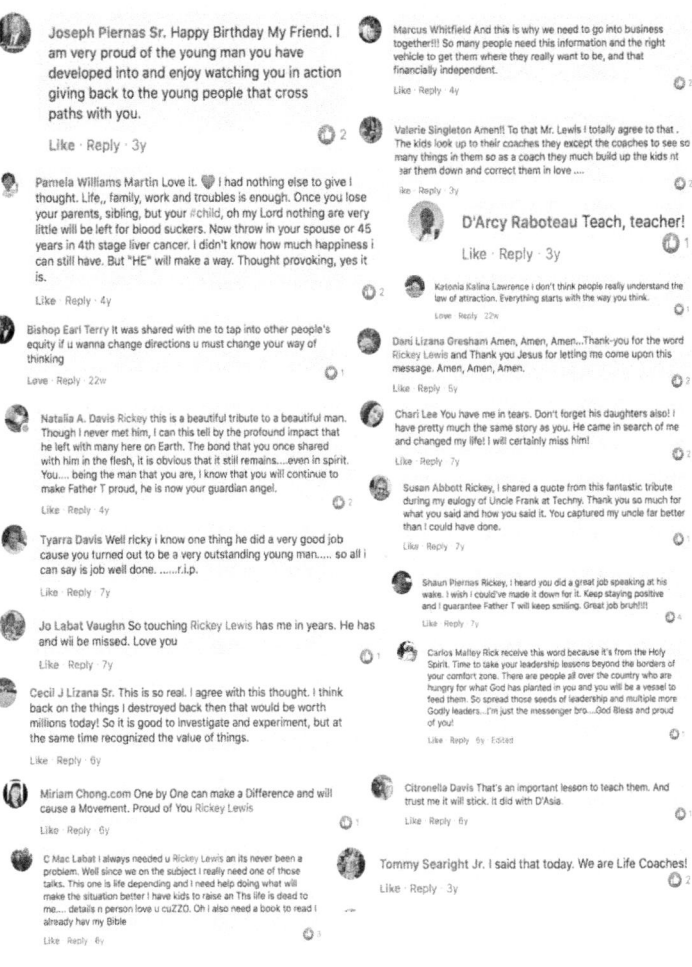

Joseph Piernas Sr. Happy Birthday My Friend. I am very proud of the young man you have developed into and enjoy watching you in action giving back to the young people that cross paths with you.
Like · Reply · 3y

Pamela Williams Martin Love it. 💜 I had nothing else to give I thought. Life,, family, work and troubles is enough. Once you lose your parents, sibling, but your #child, oh my Lord nothing are very little will be left for blood suckers. Now throw in your spouse or 45 years in 4th stage liver cancer. I didn't know how much happiness i can still have. But "HE" will make a way. Thought provoking, yes it is.
Like · Reply · 4y

Bishop Earl Terry It was shared with me to tap into other people's equity if u wanna change directions u must change your way of thinking
Love · Reply · 22w

Natalia A. Davis Rickey this is a beautiful tribute to a beautiful man. Though I never met him, I can this tell by the profound impact that he left with many here on Earth. The bond that you once shared with him in the flesh, it is obvious that it still remains....even in spirit. You.... being the man that you are, I know that you will continue to make Father T proud, he is now your guardian angel.
Like · Reply · 4y

Tyarra Davis Well ricky i know one thing he did a very good job cause you turned out to be a very outstanding young man..... so all i can say is job well done. ......r.i.p.
Like · Reply · 7y

Jo Labat Vaughn So touching Rickey Lewis has me in years. He has and wii be missed. Love you
Like · Reply · 7y

Cecil J Lizana Sr. This is so real. I agree with this thought. I think back on the things I destroyed back then that would be worth millions today! So it is good to investigate and experiment, but at the same time recognized the value of things.
Like · Reply · 6y

Miriam Chong.com One by One can make a Difference and will cause a Movement. Proud of You Rickey Lewis
Like · Reply · 6y

C Mac Labat I always needed u Rickey Lewis an its never been a problem. Well since we on the subject I really need one of those talks. This one is life depending and I need help doing what will make the situation better I have kids to raise an Ths life is dead to me.... details n person love u cuZZO. Oh I also need a book to read I already hav my Bible
Like · Reply · 6y

Marcus Whitfield And this is why we need to go into business together!!! So many people need this information and the right vehicle to get them where they really want to be, and that financially independent.
Like · Reply · 4y

Valerie Singleton Amen!! To that Mr. Lewis I totally agree to that . The kids look up to their coaches they except the coaches to see so many things in them so as a coach they much build up the kids nt ʒar them down and correct them in love ....
ike · Reply · 3y

D'Arcy Raboteau Teach, teacher!
Like · Reply · 3y

Katonia Kalina Lawrence i don't think people really understand the law of attraction. Everything starts with the way you think.
Love · Reply · 22w

Dani Lizana Gresham Amen, Amen, Amen...Thank-you for the word Rickey Lewis and Thank you Jesus for letting me come upon this message. Amen, Amen, Amen.
Like · Reply · 5y

Chari Lee You have me in tears. Don't forget his daughters also! I have pretty much the same story as you. He came in search of me and changed my life! I will certainly miss him!
Like · Reply · 7y

Susan Abbett Rickey, I shared a quote from this fantastic tribute during my eulogy of Uncle Frank at Techny. Thank you so much for what you said and how you said it. You captured my uncle far better than I could have done.
Like · Reply · 7y

Shaun Piernas Rickey, I heard you did a great job speaking at his wake. I wish I could've made it down for it. Keep staying positive and I guarantee Father T will keep smiling. Great job bruh!!!
Like · Reply · 7y

Carlos Malley Rick receive this word because it's from the Holy Spirit. Time to take your leadership lessons beyond the borders of your comfort zone. There are people all over the country who are hungry for what God has planted in you and you will be a vessel to feed them. So spread those seeds of leadership and multiple more Godly leaders...I'm just the messenger bro....God bless and proud of you!
Like · Reply · 5y · Edited

Citronella Davis That's an important lesson to teach them. And trust me it will stick. It did with D'Asia.
Like · Reply · 6y

Tommy Searight Jr. I said that today. We are Life Coaches!
Like · Reply · 3y

Thank You.
Each and every one of you gave me energy and life.

Shenea Kissy Bell Loved this post as well!! Citronella and I talked about your Positive, Encouraging post last week!! They are helpful and encouraging...keep them coming!!! I Love the analogy of life and the building that you use!!!....you should put that on a poster!!! Perhaps you should put these posts in a book and publish it!!!;it's really that good!!!!
Like · Reply · 7y

Made in the USA
Middletown, DE
02 July 2020